D0308998

Motorcycle Roadcraft

THE POLICE RIDER'S HANDBOOK TO BETTER MOTORCYCLING

The Stationery Office
London

Author: Philip Coyne
Design and illustration: Bill Mayblin
Editor: Penny Mares
Research: Philip Coyne, Bill Mayblin, Penny Mares

The author and working group wish to acknowledge the contribution of Dr Robert West to the contents of Chapter 1.

The Police Foundation

The Police Foundation is an independent research charity working to improve the effectiveness of policing and the relationship between the police and the communities they serve.

For further details of the Foundation's work and publications contact:

The Police Foundation
1 Glyn Street
London SE11 5RA

Tel: 0207 582 3744
Fax: 0207 587 0671
UK Charity No: 278257

National Extension College

The National Extension College is an educational trust and a registered charity with a distinguished body of trustees. It is an independent, self-financing organisation. Since it was established in 1963, NEC has pioneered the development of flexible learning for adults. NEC is actively developing innovative materials and systems for distance learning opportunities on over 100 courses, from basic skills and general education to degree and professional training.

For further details of NEC's resources and courses contact:

Customer Services Department
National Extension College
18 Brooklands Avenue
Cambridge CB2 2HN

Tel: 01223 316644
Fax: 01223 313586

© Police Foundation 1996

Applications for reproduction should be made in writing to
The Stationery Office, St. Crispins, Duke Street, Norwich NR3 1PD

Fourth impression 2000

ISBN 0 11 341143 X

Printed in the United Kingdom for The Stationery Office by MPS Shrewsbury

TJ000580 3/00 C70

Acknowledgements

This new edition of *Motorcycle Roadcraft* was initiated by The Police Foundation at the request of the Association of Chief Police Officers. It was produced by the National Police Driving Schools' Conference Motorcycle Roadcraft Working Party in conjunction with the Police Foundation and the National Extension College.

The Police Foundation would like to thank the many individuals and organisations who gave so freely of their time and expertise in the preparation of this edition of *Motorcycle Roadcraft*.

This edition of *Motorcycle Roadcraft* has been approved by the Association of Chief Police Officers, which is satisfied that it reflects current best practice in police rider instruction and takes into account the relevant views of civilian experts.

Other essential guides to safe driving also published by The Stationery Office include:

Roadcraft – The Police Driver's Handbook
(011 340 8587)

Roadcraft Video – The Police Driver's Course on Advanced Driving
(011 341 1308)

Towing Roadcraft – The Essential Towing Handbook
(011 552 1917)

To order or find out more about these or any other driving titles, telephone The Stationery Office customer service on 0870 600 5522

Contents

Chapter 3

Observation

Chapter 4

Acceleration, using gears and braking

Chapter 5
Cornering, balance and avoiding skids 85

Chapter 6
Signals 107

About *Motorcycle Roadcraft*

How can *Motorcycle Roadcraft* help your riding?

The aim of *Motorcycle Roadcraft* is to improve the skill and safety of your riding so that you can make the best use of road and traffic conditions. Riding safety and riding skill are aspects of the same ability – the ability to control the position and speed of your bike relative to everything else on the road. An accident or even a near miss usually represents a loss of this control – a lapse in riding skill. *Motorcycle Roadcraft* aims to help you improve your skills by increasing your awareness of the range of factors that affect your riding – your own capabilities, the characteristics of your machine, and the road and traffic conditions.

Motorcycle Roadcraft is the textbook for police riders undertaking police rider training. In police training, *Motorcycle Roadcraft* is combined with practical instruction. This edition is designed so that it can be used for self study either before or during a course, and for ready reference afterwards.

What machines does *Motorcycle Roadcraft* cover?

Motorcycle Roadcraft is written with a modern motorcycle in mind but the advice it contains is relevant to both older and smaller bikes. You do, however, need to adapt your riding to the different characteristics of these machines.

The basic design and the supplementary aids built into a bike affect its handling characteristics. These vary widely between machines and it is not possible in a book of this size to cover every variation in bike geometry, traction control, linked braking or antilock braking system (ABS). To ride well you need to understand these characteristics, so it is important to know and follow the manufacturer's guidance and the advice of your instructor.

What *Motorcycle Roadcraft* does not include

Motorcycle Roadcraft assumes that you are thoroughly familiar with the current edition of the *Highway Code* and the *Know your Traffic Signs* booklet. Advice and instructions contained in these publications are not generally repeated in *Motorcycle Roadcraft*.

Special techniques, such as those used in emergency response or pursuit, are not covered in *Motorcycle Roadcraft*. We recommend that riders consult their instructors and the appropriate codes of practice for guidance in these areas. Techniques which require a high level of instructional guidance to ensure their safety have also been excluded. Your instructor will introduce you to these techniques when appropriate.

Using *Motorcycle Roadcraft* for self study

Motorcycle Roadcraft has a number of features to make it easier to use and to help you check your learning.

- At the start of each chapter there is a *Use this chapter to find out* section. This identifies the main learning points of the chapter. Use it to help you select the chapters or sections that you need to concentrate on.
- Illustrations and diagrams are used to explain complex ideas. They are an essential part of the book and often contain information not explained elsewhere.
- Key points are *highlighted in colour.*
- Throughout the text you will find questions and activities. These are designed to help you check your understanding and assess your progress. Many of the activities are practical, helping you to transfer the advice in *Motorcycle Roadcraft* to your everyday riding.
- At the end of each chapter there is a review of the key points and questions to help you check your understanding.

We suggest that you keep a notebook for making your own notes and for completing the written activities. This will help you to organise your work and will provide a readily available record for reviewing your own progress.

Working through the chapters

Chapters 1, 2 and 3 set out the basic principles and information on which later chapters build, so ideally you should read these first. If you are using *Motorcycle Roadcraft* as part of a riding course, consult your instructor who may want you to study certain sections of the book in a different order.

The importance of practice

Just reading *Motorcycle Roadcraft* will not make you a better rider. Practice is an essential part of learning any skill. What matters is not how well you can recall the content of this book but how well you can apply what you have learnt to your riding. Many of the techniques explained in *Motorcycle Roadcraft* are fairly simple in themselves. Finesse in riding skill comes from applying them consistently. All the techniques depend on judgement and this only comes with practice. Many of the activities designed to help you practise techniques can be carried out during your everyday riding. Your goal should be to apply the techniques in *Motorcycle Roadcraft* systematically so that they become an everyday part of your riding.

You cannot absorb all the information in *Motorcycle Roadcraft* in one reading, so we suggest that you read a section, select a technique, practise it, assess your progress, and then refer back to *Motorcycle Roadcraft* to refine the technique further. The text has been designed to help you do this.

Using *Motorcycle Roadcraft* for reference

Each chapter contains cross-references to relevant information in other chapters and there is an index to make it easier to find the information that you want. There is also a glossary which explains unfamiliar terms.

Learning is a continuous process

Being a good rider means that you never stop learning. To improve your skills you must be prepared to take responsibility for your own learning. This means that you need to constantly review and, where necessary, adapt your riding to maintain standards and improve techniques. Motorcycles and riding conditions are constantly changing, and your skills need to keep pace with these changes, otherwise they will become outdated, inappropriate and dangerous. Whenever you ride, regard it as an opportunity to reassess and improve your skills. Only by constantly developing your insight and knowledge can you fulfil your responsibility to ride safely and effectively.

Use this chapter to find out:

- the characteristics of a good rider
- the risks of having an accident and how to reduce them
- why attitude is so important
- how to recognise and cope with red mist
- how to set about changing inappropriate attitudes
- how to stay alert and what to do about fatigue
- the importance of riding defensively
- how to learn riding skills.

Chapter 1

Becoming a better rider

The mental characteristics of a good rider

This chapter is about how you can become a better rider. It focuses not on the physical but on the mental aspects of riding skills, and looks at how attitudes and concentration affect riding performance.

Research evidence shows that attitudes affect riding safety, but developing appropriate attitudes is not simple. It depends on recognising that attitudes are important, and on making a personal commitment to changing attitudes that are unsafe. The first part of the chapter looks at what makes a good rider. It goes on to look at the pattern of traffic accidents in Great Britain, and at what the research evidence tells us about who is at greatest risk of having an accident. Understanding this evidence can be an important step in recognising and changing inappropriate attitudes.

What makes a good rider?

Good riders have a quiet efficiency in their actions and this derives from:

- a good level of concentration
- accurate observation
- matching the machine's speed and direction to the situation
- awareness of the risks inherent in particular road and traffic situations
- acting to keep identified risks to a minimum
- awareness of their own limitations and those of the machine and the road
- skilful use of machine controls
- attitudes that contribute to road safety.

It is not simply the speed of your reactions that determines whether you are a safe rider but your ability to identify and respond to hazards. Being able to respond quickly to simple stimuli such as noise and light does not in itself reduce accident risks. Young, inexperienced riders typically have very fast reactions to simple stimuli but have slow reactions to traffic hazards.

The ability to detect hazards is learnt like any other skill and depends partly on experience. More-experienced riders develop a sensitivity to the early indications of possible trouble. When risks arise they monitor them at a subconscious level in readiness to respond quickly if the situation develops dangerously. Because they are more aware of potential danger they are more alert while riding, and this helps to sustain their concentration. (For more on concentration and attention see below.)

Traffic accidents

Most riders think they are both safer and more skilful than the average rider – but we cannot all be right. In more than 90% of traffic accidents, human error is the cause; accidents do not just happen by chance, they are the consequence of unsafe riding practices. Riding safety cannot be thought of as an add-on extra; it has to be built into the way you ride.

Road accidents

Traffic accidents account for:

- almost half of all accidental deaths in Britain
- nearly a quarter of all adult deaths under 30, whether accidental or not – they are the largest single cause of death for young adults.

Your likelihood of having an accident

Average car drivers cover about 10,000 miles a year and have a one in seven chance of an accident during that time. Compared with drivers, the risk for motorcyclists is much greater. They are:

- more than 35 times more likely to be killed or seriously injured
- eight times more likely to be involved in an accident which results in injury
- 20 times more likely to be injured themselves.

Riders who have a greater than average risk of having an accident are:

- those travelling more miles than average per year
- younger riders, especially men
- inexperienced riders.

Who is most likely to be involved in a motorcycle accident?

Statistics show that, overwhelmingly, it is young, inexperienced males who are most likely to be involved in a motorcycle accident:

- 93% of riders involved in injury accidents are male
- the peak age for being killed on a motorbike is 17
- comparing riders aged 20 and riders aged 30 with the same riding experience, the 20 year olds have three times the accident risk of the 30 year olds
- comparing riders of the same age, those in their first year of riding have a three times greater risk of accident than those in their sixth year of riding
- the average rider starting at 17 will have had more than eight accidents by the age of 35.

What are the likeliest sorts of accidents?

We can also tell from the statistics which are the commonest types of motorcycle accident:

- three-quarters of accidents occur in built-up areas
- just over half the fatalities occur in non-built-up areas
- 15% of accidents occur during overtaking
- 12% of accidents occur during cornering
- 30% of accidents in wet weather involve a skid.

Do we learn from our mistakes?

Riders at risk

Sadly the evidence shows that we do not learn very well from our mistakes. Even after taking account of age, sex, annual mileage and riding experience, some riders are consistently more at risk than others:

- riders who have had an accident in the previous three years are three times more likely than average to have an accident in the following year.

We know that drivers tend to repeat the same type of accident and the same is likely to be true for riders. If you have an accident or near miss you should think very carefully about what you could have done to avoid the situation. If you do not learn from your experience you are likely to repeat the same mistakes.

Riding too close

The practice of riding too close to the vehicle in front gives a valuable insight into the way accidents happen. Because errors go unpunished – that is, they are not always followed by an accident – they develop into bad habits which increase the risk that one day the rider will be involved in an accident.

Riding too close to the vehicle in front is a double risk for a rider because it does not allow sufficient space to compensate for a driver behind who is also too close. Driving too close is one of the commonest causes of vehicle accidents. Riders should recognise this characteristic of drivers and compensate by increasing their own following distance. A rear shunt is dangerous for a rider at whatever speed.

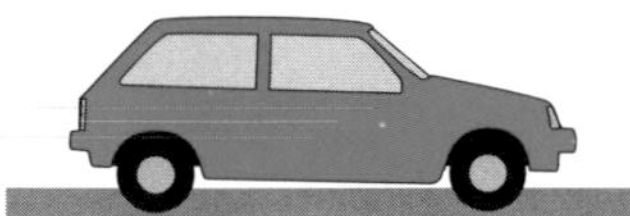

Driving too close to the vehicle in front is one of the commonest causes of accidents. It is so common that most riders see no risk in it. Half the rear end shunts occur when the vehicle in front brakes sharply and the one behind does not stop in time.

Resistance to learning from experience

These facts show that we are not very good at learning from experience. Most riders involved in an accident do not accept that they contributed to it. If you think that you did not help to cause an accident, you will also think that you have nothing to learn from it, and your riding technique, together with any faults that contributed to the accident, will remain unchanged.

To become a better rider, we have to recognise the resistance in ourselves to accepting responsibility, and take steps to overcome it. The first step is to recognise that we all have a resistance to learning. **Once we have learnt to do something routinely we are very reluctant to alter that routine, whatever the evidence that it does not work.**

Every near miss and accident needs to be seen as an opportunity to re-evaluate and improve your riding technique.

Have you experienced a near miss or accident?

Have you been involved in a near miss or accident in the last three years?

☐ yes ☐ no

If the answer is yes, did the incident involve:

☐ a rear end shunt?
☐ following too closely?
☐ a vehicle driving across your priority?
☐ losing control of your machine?

Did the incident involve a rider/driver (that might include you) in one of the higher than average risk categories:

☐ a rider/driver covering more miles than average per year?
☐ a male rider/driver?
☐ a younger rider/driver?
☐ an inexperienced rider/driver?

What have you learnt from the experience?

An ability to be self-critical and learn from experience is one of the key attributes of a good rider. The next sections look at other positive and negative attitudes that influence riding skill.

How attitude affects good riding

How would you describe your attitude

to other road users?

to speed?

to risk taking?

Studies have shown that riders' attitudes to other road users, speed and risk taking are a good guide to their likelihood of having an accident. Later in this section there is an opportunity for you to try two examples of attitude tests used in research studies.

Attitudes to other road users

Good riding depends on constructive attitudes and consideration for other road users. There is already a great deal of potential conflict on the roads without adding to it by selfish and aggressive behaviour. Such behaviour increases the stress levels of other road users and increases the risk of accidents. Many road users become unnecessarily angry when others interrupt their progress. Even behaviour that is perfectly reasonable may be a source of irritation. Riders should be aware that their ability to filter through slower moving traffic may cause some drivers to react angrily. You can reduce the risk of accidents for yourself and everyone else by being more tolerant and by avoiding actions which create unnecessary stress. Riders who show consideration for other road users are less likely themselves to become involved in accidents.

Attitudes to speed

The speed at which you ride is one of the most important factors in determining your risk of having an accident. Riding too fast is probably the factor that puts riders at greatest risk of fatality. The faster you go, the less chance you have of taking avoiding action, and the greater your risk of having an accident. Speed is largely a matter of choice – the occasions when it is absolutely necessary to ride fast are fairly limited. Good riding requires you to ride at a speed that is safe for the conditions.

Attitudes to risk taking

There is always some degree of risk while riding a motorcycle, but a rider's attitudes can greatly influence the risk involved. A general acceptance of risk is associated with a higher risk of an accident while riding. Attitudes which predispose you to risk are:

- enjoying the thrill of danger
- enjoying impressing other road users
- a disregard for personal safety
- the illusion of control, or overestimating your ability
- 'noble cause' risk taking.

Young, inexperienced riders run the greatest risk of accidents because they have a greater tendency to seek risk and disregard danger. They also see less risk in many traffic situations than more experienced riders.

Motorcyclists who ignore the law and ride in a risky way think that the risk of having an accident is lower than other riders do. In fact the risk of an accident for this group is higher than it is for other riders.

Many riders take risks to impress other people – for example, young male riders tend to ride faster when they have a young male passenger than when alone or with a female passenger.

Riders tend to suffer from the illusion of control, which is a tendency to overestimate their ability to cope with the demands of traffic when they are riding. This undermines the accurate perception of risk.

Police riders, like riders in the other emergency services, need to be aware that risks cannot be justified by telling themselves that they are taking the risks in a noble cause – to help someone else, or to catch a person suspected of a crime. Your overriding responsibility in any situation is to ride safely, and that is what you should be thinking about while you are riding to an emergency. If you have an accident and you fail to arrive, you are no help to the people in need. If you injure yourself or someone else on the way you will have turned an emergency into a tragedy, and will still have done nothing to help. Your objective should be to arrive as quickly as is safely possible, and *Motorcycle Roadcraft* is designed to help you do that.

Time pressure and the purpose of your journey

Police riders are trained to respond to urgent calls without taking undue risks. It is nevertheless a fact that riders who feel their journey is urgent, either because of time pressure or because of the purpose of the journey, tend to respond less safely to hazards and take more risks. A sense of urgency does not give the right to take risks. No emergency is so great that it justifies the possibility of injuring or killing someone through bad riding. It is better to arrive late than not at all.

Red mist

'Red mist' is the term used to describe the state of mind of riders who are so determined to achieve some objective – catching a vehicle in front, getting to an incident in the shortest possible time, overtaking another road user – that they are no longer capable of realistically assessing riding risks. Their mind is not on their riding but on some other goal; they have become emotionally and physiologically caught up in the chase. Red mist can affect all road users, but riders in the emergency services need to be particularly aware of the problem. This section focuses on the needs of police riders, but other riders may also find it helpful.

Riders suffering from red mist tend to ignore normal risk factors such as wet roads, heavy traffic or urban conditions, and the outcome is a significant increase in accidents. It is important to recognise that this happens as much in short pursuits at relatively low speeds as in fast motorway pursuits. It is a significant problem which riders need to take steps to avoid.

To prevent red mist, riders need to be able to maintain their usual calm, considered approach when responding to emergencies. The key to this is to concentrate on the riding task in hand rather than on the incident. Above all, avoid thinking about what is happening at the scene of the incident, or personalizing the conflict with the road user you are pursuing.

Individuals vary in the strategy they use to help them concentrate on riding in these situations. Some riders find that deciding to think only about their riding is enough. Others remind themselves of the horrific consequences of risk taking, or that the incident they are responding to is at least ten minutes old and will have changed, no matter how quickly they arrive. Each rider has to find their own method of keeping calm and concentrating, but the key steps in helping to prevent red mist are set out below.

- Do not get into a personality conflict with the person you are pursuing. Be dispassionate about the task and concentrate on behaviour rather than personality. Use deliberately neutral, non-aggressive language to describe the other person (to yourself as well as to others).
- Do not imagine what you are likely to find at the incident – assess the incident when you arrive at it.
- Concentrate on your riding – if you find this difficult, try giving yourself a running commentary on your riding, spoken aloud.

Other causes of risk taking

Greater risk taking also arises from attitudes that have nothing directly to do with risk assessment. Impatient, aggressive and selfish attitudes in drivers are linked with excessive speed and a tendency to commit driving violations that put them at risk. Also a disregard for social values (such as defrauding insurance companies, illegal parking, tax evasion, not paying TV licences and a general disregard for the law) has been specifically identified with an increased risk of accident. The same is likely to apply to motorcyclists. We know that riders who commit violations and ride in a risky manner have a greater than average risk of accident.

Rash decision making also increases the risk. If you do not consider all the implications of your decisions, your actions are unpredictable and you fail to take account of traffic conditions.

Emotional mood and accident risk

Road users commonly express how they feel in the way that they ride/drive, and this can be very dangerous. Road users who have recently had an argument behave more aggressively than normal and ride/drive too fast and too close to the vehicle in front. American research shows that there is a greater risk of an accident during times of stress such as during divorce proceedings.

Traffic delays are a common source of stress and frustration. Many riders release this anger by riding more aggressively and by taking more risks. If you are able to recognise this as a problem and can find other ways of coping with the stress you will improve your riding. Focusing on the present rather than on the purpose of the journey is one way of reducing the stress.

How do mood and stress affect your riding?

Can you pinpoint things that may have affected your mood while riding during the past week, for example:

☐ a source of long-term or serious stress in your life?

☐ an argument or other incident causing you short-term stress?

☐ daily sources of frustration in the journeys you make?

How often do you get angry with other road users?

☐ Never ☐ Rarely ☐ Sometimes ☐ Quite often ☐ Very often

How does anger affect your behaviour?

Has your anger ever resulted in a confrontation?

What in the past have you done to control your anger?

Attitudes and society

Our attitudes are shaped to a large degree by the society which we live in, the organisations we belong to and the company we keep. These groups help us to define what is normal, what is acceptable and what is desirable. We take on the attitudes of those with whom we identify. This is partly because it helps us to feel good about ourselves and partly because we look for approval from those whose views we care about.

Large organisations can affect attitudes to road safety through educational and publicity material. They can adopt policies that reward safe riding and punish unsafe riding. This is why it is particularly important that police riders are seen to be exemplary riders. The attitude that police riders take towards their riding will be noticed by society at large and will influence other riders. Police riders should always be aware that they are seen as role models.

Because the attitudes of your colleagues and the organisation you work for affect your riding, you should be aware of what these attitudes are. Certain attitudes – for example, an overemphasis on reaching destinations on time, valuing speed and competitiveness, or using language which stereotypes or is aggressive – may undermine safe riding practices. Problems such as these really need to be dealt with at an organisational level, but the first step in remedying them is to acknowledge that they exist and that they have a personal relevance.

You need to be aware of the social influences on attitudes and safety but, in the end, the responsibility for the safety of yourself and other road users is yours alone. It is particularly important to be aware of your individual responsibility for safety when riding in a group. There is a temptation to follow the leader and not to make an individual assessment of riding hazards. This is dangerous, because you alone can assess when it is safe to move and at what speed.

Most people are reactive; if they encounter another rider with a courteous attitude and an obvious concern for safety, they are encouraged to adopt a similar approach. Riders who have a professional attitude to riding and safety can influence the behaviour of other motorists for the better.

Changing unhelpful attitudes

Develop positive attitudes

We have now looked at riding attitudes that increase the risk of accidents. Positive attitudes that help reduce accident risk are:

- a tolerance and consideration for other road users
- a realistic appraisal of your own abilities
- an awareness of your vulnerability as a rider
- a high degree of care for your own safety, for your passengers and for other road users.

You need to be able to recognise your own limitations and to set aside personal goals in the interests of safety – an example would be restraining yourself from reacting aggressively to another road user's aggressive behaviour. You need to make decisions carefully, to take full account of the traffic conditions and to avoid acting in an unpredictable way.

Recognise that attitudes affect safety

Understanding your own attitudes and changing them to reduce accident risk is a difficult task. The first stage is to be aware of the effect that your attitudes can have on your riding safety. One way of gaining some insight into this is the use of attitude tests. By answering a few simple questions you can gain some idea of your attitudes and a measure of your accident risk.

Research evidence shows that well-designed attitude tests give an accurate indication of an individual's likely accident rate. The questionnaire on the next page is an example of this type of test. The actual number of accidents for any given rider will depend on many things, but questionnaires of this kind reflect the way that people ride and accurately predict the risk of having an accident.

Check your own attitudes

Use the questionnaire on the next page to assess your attitude to riding. Try and be as truthful as possible – the more truthful you are the more accurate the result will be.

Attitudes to riding

Listed below are some statements about riding. For each one show how far you agree or disagree with it by putting a circle around the appropriate number. For example circling 1 means that you strongly agree with the statement.

	Strongly agree	Agree	Neither agree nor disagree	Disagree	Strongly disagree
Decreasing the speed limit on motorways is a good idea	1	2	3	4	5
Even at night-time on quiet roads it is important to keep within the speed limit	1	2	3	4	5
Riders who cause accidents by reckless riding should be banned from riding for life	1	2	3	4	5
People should drive slower than the limit when it is raining	1	2	3	4	5
Road users should never overtake on the inside lane even if a slow driver is blocking the outside lane	1	2	3	4	5
Penalties for speeding should be more severe	1	2	3	4	5
In towns where there are a lot of pedestrians, the speed limit should be 20 mph	1	2	3	4	5

When you have finished add up the numbers which you have circled. If you scored less than 15 you tend to agree with the statements. If you scored between 15 and 21 you are generally neutral or average. If you scored more than 21 you tend to disagree with the statements. Drivers who tend to disagree with these statements turn out to have approximately five times the accident risk of those who agree.

If the table shows you to have a high accident risk, you need to think seriously about what you can do to change the attitudes that put you at risk. The next section analyses some of these attitudes and suggests how you might begin to tackle them.

Acknowledge resistance to change

Most riders would accept that developing a safety conscious attitude is important, but a problem exists because we believe our own attitudes are right and are reluctant to accept evidence that we need to change them. Attitude to speed is a key area where there is often resistance to change. To assess your own attitude to speed, complete the questionnaire that follows.

Riding speed

For each question put a circle around the number corresponding to the answer that applies to you during your normal everyday riding (not during emergency riding).

	Never or very infrequently	Quite infrequently	Infrequently	Frequently	Always
How often do you exceed the 70 mph limit during a motorway journey?	1	2	3	4	5
How often do you exceed the speed limit in built-up areas?	1	2	3	4	5
How often do you ride fast?	1	2	3	4	5

When you have finished, you can add up the numbers which you have circled. If you scored less than 7, you tend to speed infrequently. If you scored between 7 and 12 you tend to speed a little more frequently. If you scored more than 12 you tend to speed often. Drivers who indicate on this questionnaire that they speed often have about three times the accident risk of those who speed infrequently.

If you have scored more than 12 on the questionnaire do you agree that you have a greater risk of causing an accident? Or do you think there are mitigating circumstances in your case?

If the latter, make a list of these mitigating circumstances and then decide whether they are genuinely mitigating or whether they spring from a reluctance to accept change.

Discussing this with a colleague could help to make your assessment more objective.

Many riders who are fast, aggressive and inconsiderate are quite happy with the way they ride and do not accept that it is unsafe. They tend to think that their behaviour is more common than it really is, and that it is the result of external pressures rather than their own choice. These rationalisations create barriers to attitude change, and need to be challenged to allow scope for change.

Recognise your own vulnerability

If you have inappropriate attitudes towards riding, and are able to acknowledge this, the next step is to identify safety as your primary concern. Consider the elements that bolster your unsafe riding attitudes and how you can change them. Most important amongst these are:

- a false sense of personal invulnerability
- an illusion of control.

See **Riding defensively**, page 21.

These attitudes tend to prevent us from accepting that the risks of riding apply to us as well as to other people.

Critical self-awareness – the key to riding skill

Acknowledging the need to change attitudes is difficult because the evidence is statistical and most people trust their own experience rather than statistics. If you are a fast or aggressive rider, you may not make the connection between your attitudes and the way you ride even if you have been in an accident. Research has shown that riders have a strong tendency to blame the road conditions or other road users rather than themselves for the accidents that they cause. This helps to explain why there is a strong tendency for riders repeatedly to make the same mistakes and become involved in the same kinds of accidents.

A fully professional approach to riding requires you to take an objective look at the facts, to be prepared, where there is evidence, to discard inappropriate attitudes and to develop a critical awareness of your own attitudes and capabilities.

The key steps to achieving this critical self-awareness are:

- acknowledging that attitudes affect riding performance
- being aware of your own attitudes and recognising that they affect your risk of having an accident
- recognising that you are vulnerable, especially on a motorcycle
- making safety your primary concern in all your riding decisions
- considering your own experience of near misses or accidents and what you can learn from them
- carrying through changes in attitude to your riding performance by applying them in every riding situation.

Concentration and alertness

Concentration and alertness are also key mental aspects of riding skill. This section looks at the factors which can help or hinder them.

Our ability to handle information about the environment is limited. We cope with this by giving more attention to some parts of the environment than others and concentrating on them. This is important in riding because we react most quickly to things happening in the part of the environment on which we are concentrating.

One way of seeing this is to imagine your field of view as a picture – you can see the whole picture but you can only concentrate on one part of it at a time.

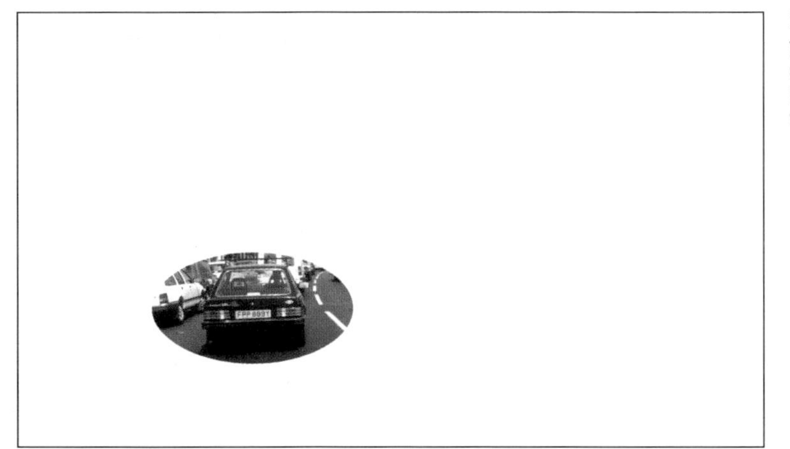

If you concentrate your vision on a small area you are less aware of the whole picture.

If you concentrate on different areas of the environment in turn, you become more aware of the picture as a whole.

Scanning the environment

Riders who can rapidly scan the whole environment looking for different kinds of hazards have a lower risk of accident than riders who concentrate on one area. There are several ways you can develop your ability to do this:

- move your eyes around and look in all directions, including the mirrors
- look for hazards in any shape or size and from any direction
- develop your sensitivity to the variety of possible hazards in different riding situations – this depends on learning, experience and a commitment to developing this awareness.

Riders have observational advantages over car drivers in that they are generally sitting higher and have greater flexibility in positioning their machine to get a good view. If properly used, these observational advantages can help to offset the rider's greater vulnerability.

In looking for cars and lorries, riders can become blind to smaller, less expected road users.

Looking but not seeing

What we see depends to a large extent on what we expect to see. You may have experienced, at one time or another, pulling out and narrowly missing a bicycle coming from the direction in which you have just looked. Errors of this type are common because road users, including riders, are generally looking for cars or lorries but not for smaller objects such as bicycles or motorcycles, which they fail to see. When we concentrate, we don't just look at a particular part of a scene, we look for particular types of objects in that scene. We find it easier to detect objects that we expect to see, and react more quickly to them. Conversely we often fail to see objects that we do not expect to see. This has important implications for your safety as a rider.

See *Riding defensively*, page 21.

Developing your hazard awareness

Some processing of information goes on at a subconscious level but a prompt can summon our attention to it. An example is the way we prick up our ears when we hear our name mentioned. Experienced riders rapidly and automatically switch their attention to events happening outside their field of focus because they have a subconscious or instinctive understanding of the implications of particular traffic situations.

In the following chapters of *Motorcycle Roadcraft* we analyse many examples of traffic situations for the hazards that occur in them. You may wonder whether so many examples are necessary, but their purpose is to increase your understanding of the potential hazards in each situation. The aim is to 'pre-sensitise' your awareness so that when you encounter a situation you already know what hazards to look for and can respond to them more quickly.

Alertness

Alertness determines the amount of information you can process – it can be thought of as mental energy and its opposite is tiredness or fatigue. Alertness depends on many things, but with routine tasks like riding, it tends to decrease with time spent on the task. Alertness also depends to some extent on your personality. Extroverts (outgoing people who need a lot of external stimulation) are probably more susceptible to fatigue than introverts (inward-looking people who avoid high levels of stimulation).

To ride well we need to remain alert – ready to anticipate, identify and respond to hazards. But most riding is routine; it places few demands on our abilities and the risk of accidents from moment to moment is small. This relatively low level of stimulation makes it easy to lose concentration, and we need to take active steps to maintain it. In busy urban traffic, the demands of riding may be sufficiently stimulating, but on long journeys on motorways or rural roads other forms of stimulation are needed.

Alertness and anxiety

Alertness depends on your level of anxiety, and there is an optimum level of anxiety for any task. A small amount of anxiety arising from a sound understanding of the risks involved can help to maintain alertness and readiness to respond. No anxiety at all dampens your responsiveness and decreases your speed of reaction. Too much anxiety can result in failure to process information and respond appropriately.

You can help yourself to stay alert by:

- consciously assessing the current level of risk
- constantly updating your assessment

- talking yourself through the risks of the traffic situation.

If you actively maintain your awareness of the risks in this way, it will help you to keep anxiety at an optimum level, and you will be less likely to neglect a potentially dangerous situation.

Fatigue

Fatigue is related to the total time spent at work and not just to the time spent on the machine. If you are tired from other duties before you start a journey, you are much more at risk from fatigue during the journey. Riders have an increased susceptibility to fatigue because of noise, vibration and exposure to wind and weather. Professional riders are particularly at risk because professional and social pressures encourage them to continue riding beyond what they know is their safe limit.

Health, medication and emotional state

You should not ride when you feel unwell. This is particularly important on motorways because of the dangers of high-speed accidents and the limited opportunities to stop if you feel ill. Medication is a common source of drowsiness, so if you are taking medicine follow any advice on the container or given by your doctor about riding. Your emotional state affects your ability to recognise hazards, to take appropriate decisions and to implement them efficiently. If you are emotionally distressed you should be aware of the effect that it is likely to have on your riding.

Monotonous conditions

Riding for long periods of time in monotonous conditions such as low-density traffic, fog, at night or on a motorway, reduces stimulation and promotes fatigue.

How to combat fatigue

To reduce the risk of fatigue:

- make sure that you are not tired before you start riding
- use any available adjustments to make your riding position comfortable
- adopt a comfortable position on the machine with your instep resting on the foot rests

- consider wearing internal ear protectors (ear-plugs) to reduce noise
- wear clothing that provides physical protection and is appropriate to the weather.

Fatigue can be caused by both hot and cold conditions. In warm weather, light-coloured garments will help to keep you cool as well as making you more conspicuous. In wet weather, it is important to wear fully waterproof outergarments – saturated clothes remove heat from the body very quickly in the airflow of a moving bike. Remember that gloves and boots need to be waterproof also.

Cold weather is dangerous; as the body's core cools, the rider becomes sluggish and loses attention. The extremities cool more quickly than the body and in cold weather the average temperature of riders' hands is around 14 to 15 °C. At this point they lose most of their sensitivity.

Take effective action to prevent chilling by:

- wearing multiple layers – the more layers you wear the warmer you will be
- wearing a thick suit covered by an outer windproof suit
- closing all fasteners to prevent the suit from ballooning – movement of air inside a suit causes chilling
- avoiding clothes which make you sweat – sweat removes heat when it evaporates
- keeping your head, hands and feet well insulated.

Bad posture causes muscular fatigue which in turn causes mental fatigue. Emergency riding often causes tension in posture, which is also fatiguing. As far as possible, try to relax your posture during emergency riding.

At night, dazzle and constantly changing conditions of visibility quickly result in tiredness. Night riding puts heavy demands on the eyes and any slight eyesight irregularity can cause stress and fatigue. If you find you are suffering from fatigue unexpectedly, especially at night, it is wise to get your eyes tested. As we age, most of us develop eyesight irregularities and can benefit from correctly prescribed glasses.

Noise and vibration cause fatigue, so do everything possible to reduce them. Open the ventilation holes on your helmet if it helps to keep you alert, but not if it causes excessive noise or makes your head cold.

Taking rest breaks is essential to recover from the onset of fatigue. It appears that most people need a rest break of at least 20 minutes to restore alertness. On long journeys you should plan a series of rest breaks, but recognise that each successive break will give less recovery than the one before. Physical activity helps recovery, so include some walking as well as sitting down and relaxing during planned breaks.

Riders over 45 need to be aware that they are more at risk of and recover less quickly from fatigue than younger riders.

Biological rhythms

Alertness is reduced if you ride at times when you would normally be asleep or if you have not had a normal amount of sleep. It also varies with the time of day;

- our reactions tend to be slightly faster in the early evening than in the morning
- there seems to be a dip in alertness after the midday meal
- the greatest risk of fatigue-related accidents is between the hours of midnight and 8.00 am.

Irregular work and shift patterns also increase the risk of fatigue.

If you feel drowsy, if your eyelids are heavy and the rear lights ahead start to blur, you must do something to stop yourself falling asleep. Take a rest as soon as it is safe.

Riding defensively

Riders are extremely vulnerable. Unlike car drivers they have no protective shell around them, their stability is highly dependent on the quality of the road surface, they are not very conspicuous and other drivers take greater risks when pulling out in front of them. Set against this, riders have advantages in observation, positioning and acceleration.

Conspicuity (being more easily seen)

One-third of drivers involved in a daylight collision with a motorcyclist claim not to have seen the rider before the accident. At night this figure rises to over half of all drivers. The head-on view of a rider and machine is relatively small, presenting a small image from which to assess speed. If the situation is busy it can be difficult to distinguish a machine and rider against the background and we saw earlier that many drivers have a blind spot when it comes to looking for riders. At night riders face more difficulties: the headlight is often insufficiently bright to attract attention, it may become 'lost' among the confusion of other headlights and because it is only one light, it provides a poor cue for assessing speed and distance.

You should do everything you can to make yourself more conspicuous. You can do this by:

- wearing a jacket or over-vest that is fluorescent and has reflective markings
- using daylight running lights
- using a bright quartz halogen headlamp.

If your machine is fitted with daylight running lights, use them. If not, use a dipped headlight instead. Tests have shown that the combination of a fluorescent jacket or vest and a 55W quartz halogen headlamp makes riders significantly more conspicuous.

In making your riding plan you should always take into account your conspicuousness, and consider how well you stand out against the background. Be aware that this can change rapidly: a white machine against black tarmac is relatively visible, for example, but the same machine against a white lorry merges into the background. Do not assume that because you are conspicuous you are safe. As always your safety depends on the quality of your observation and planning.

Three-quarters of the accidents where the driver claims not to have seen the rider occur at junctions. You should approach junctions at which there is a waiting or approaching vehicle with considerable caution. Reduce speed until you are sure that the other road user is aware of your presence and follow the advice in the chapters on observation and positioning.

See Chapter 3, ***Observation*** *and Chapter 7,* ***Positioning****.*

Clothing

Clothing is currently the main protection available to a rider in an accident. A helmet must be in good condition, as even the slightest damage can severely reduce its strength. It should be correctly fitted – the padding and straps should be adjusted so that it does not move once it is on the head.

Outer clothing should be flexible, resistant to abrasion, and provide a degree of support; it should have padding on key areas such as elbows, knees and shoulders. Leather is generally regarded as the most suitable material. Boots should be worn to protect the foot, ankle and lower leg and gloves to protect the hands. Brightly coloured or fluorescent clothing with reflective panels will help to improve conspicuity.

Noise from a bike causes fatigue in the short term and damages your hearing in the long term. Use ear-plugs to lessen fatigue and reduce the risk of hearing damage.

Developing your ability to ride defensively

The most important thing to recognise as a rider is that your safety depends on your actions and your ability to anticipate and avoid the actions of other vehicles. You need a high level of attention, an awareness of likely hazards and excellent observational skills. You need to make the most of the advantages of height, positioning flexibility and speed that a machine provides. The ability to sense danger in a situation only develops with experience, so you should always ride well within your capabilities. Always make sure the roadspace that you intend to enter is positively safe. Remember that, even in daylight, up to a third of other road users will not even realise you are there.

Learning skills

Safe riding habits depend on appropriate attitudes and on appropriate skills in hazard perception and vehicle control. You will find it easier to improve and develop your skills if you have some understanding of how we learn skills and of what role instruction plays in the learning process.

Skilled performance of any task depends on three main elements:

- rapid and accurate perception of the relevant information
- rapid choice of an appropriate response
- accurate execution of the chosen response.

Attitude, as we have seen, is important in identifying what is relevant and in selecting what is appropriate. Speed and accuracy, the other attributes of skill, depend on practice and feedback.

Practice and feedback

The two basic requirements for skill development are practice and feedback on the effect of our actions. The better the feedback the better the learning. Complicated skills such as riding are built up from smaller skill elements. Early in practice we need detailed feedback on each of the elements but later, as the different elements of a skill are put together and become automatic, we are less and less aware of our individual actions. This has two results: firstly, each decision covers a bigger task so that fewer decisions are needed; secondly, our actions becomes smoother and less hurried.

When you have mastered the basic controls and skills required to ride a motorcycle, you can devote more of your attention to the road and traffic conditions. This improves your anticipation and response to hazards – key areas of advanced riding. Your performance becomes more relaxed and efficient, making it appear that you have all the time in the world.

Throughout this book you will find many routines, such as the system of motorcycle control, designed to improve your riding. At first they will put heavy demands on your attention and thinking time, but as you get used to them, they will become second nature. Learning roadcraft skills mirrors the process by which you learnt the basic riding skills to pass your test. At first, manoeuvres like changing gear or turning round in the road required all your attention, but with practice they became automatic, allowing you to devote more of your attention to reading the road.

There is a possible negative side to this, especially if you tend to think of riding as a mainly mechanical activity. Once a routine has been learnt, performance can become rigid and unable to respond to changing circumstances. We have already touched on this resistance to learning from experience, and it is something you need to be aware of when evaluating new approaches to old problems.

Instruction

Rider training at basic and advanced levels can accelerate your learning, enabling you to develop skills that you might otherwise never possess. Training can improve your hazard perception by making you aware of the potentially dangerous situations in different traffic environments, and by giving you practice in detecting them. But it is important for you to take an active role in developing your own learning. We each learn differently, and you alone can identify which methods work best for you. To learn effectively you need to have the right balance between instruction and practice. Instruction can draw your attention to parts of a task or ways of doing things but practice is the only way in which skills become automatic and readily available when you need them.

Overconfidence after training

In the period following training, riders can get into serious difficulties because they overestimate their new abilities. On finishing a well-supervised course your riding ability and your confidence should be in balance. As you practise the methods you have learnt there is a possibility of a mismatch developing between your actual riding ability and the confidence you have in it. There is then a danger that your confidence will take you into situations which you cannot handle, and which might result in an accident. Recognise that this is a problem you will have to tackle whenever you learn new skills. Observe your own riding critically and ride within your known limits.

The following chapters explain techniques of machine control that can help to increase your safety and reduce your risk of having an accident, but they can only do this if they are supported by positive attitudes, concentration and, above all, critical self-awareness.

Review

In this chapter we have looked at:

- the risks of having an accident
- the failure of riders to learn from experience
- the characteristics of a good rider
- how your attitudes affect your riding
- how to recognise and cope with red mist
- practical steps towards changing unsafe attitudes
- alertness, concentration and the problem of fatigue
- the importance of riding defensively
- how to develop your riding skills.

Check your understanding

What are the three types of rider that have a higher than average accident risk?

Do riders who have had an accident generally alter their riding as a result?

What are the attitudes that predispose you to risk?

Why are riders who suffer from red mist at higher risk of having an accident?

What can riders do to avoid red mist?

What can you do to stay alert?

What can you do to combat fatigue?

How can you increase your conspicuity?

How do we learn new skills?

If you have difficulty in answering any of these questions, look back over the relevant part of this chapter to refresh your memory.

Use this chapter to find out:

- the purpose of the system of motorcycle control
- what hazards are
- what the system of motorcycle control is
- how to use the system of motorcycle control
- how to apply the system to common hazards.

Chapter 2

The system of motorcycle control

The need for a system of motorcycle control

This chapter explains the system of motorcycle control, and shows you how to use the system to negotiate hazards. A feature of nearly all road accidents is human error. The purpose of the system of motorcycle control is to provide a way of approaching and negotiating hazards that is methodical, safe and leaves nothing to chance. If you use it consistently with the right frame of mind, good observation and a high level of skill in bike control, you should avoid causing accidents yourself and be able to anticipate many of the hazards caused by other road users.

Using the system will help to give you calm control of your machine, and enable you to deal with hazards without getting flustered. Your progress will be steady and unobtrusive – the characteristics of a skilled rider.

Riding skills

Riding requires more than pure handling skills. Many hazards encountered by riders are unpredictable. You need an investigative approach to recognise and negotiate them safely. You should learn to expect the unexpected. Riding uses both mental and physical skills:

Mental skills

The ability to scan the environment, recognise relevant dangers or hazards, decide on their priority and form an achievable riding plan.

Physical skills

The ability to translate intentions and thoughts into physical action accurately and smoothly.

In using these skills you need to take into account:

- real ability as opposed to perceived ability (what you can actually do as opposed to what you think you can do – in the average rider there is a significant gap between real and perceived ability. A key objective of rider training is to bring perceptions in line with reality)
- the capabilities of the machine
- the prevailing weather and road conditions.

There is much to anticipate and think about when riding. Road and traffic conditions continually change, requiring you to adjust course and speed frequently. You need to take many factors into account: the activities of other road users, where they might be and what they might do; the closeness of other vehicles; the need to signal your intentions; the road and surface conditions; the weather; and the handling characteristics of your bike. The system of motorcycle control simplifies this task. It provides a simple and consistent method of riding which ensures that you overlook no detail and leave nothing to chance.

The system of motorcycle control gives you that essential aspect of safe riding – time to react.

Hazards

A hazard is anything which is potentially dangerous. A hazard can be immediate and obvious, such as a car approaching you on the wrong side of the road, or it may be less obvious but just as potentially dangerous, such as a blind bend which conceals a lorry reversing into your path. Much of your roadcraft skill is in the early recognition of hazards – the situations that are potentially dangerous – and then taking the appropriate action to deal with them. One of the main causes of accidents is the failure to recognise hazardous situations – if you fail to see the potential danger you cannot take actions to avoid it.

See Chapter 1, **Becoming a better rider** and Chapter 3, **Observation**.

On the roads you will meet three main types of hazard:

- physical features such as junctions, roundabouts, bends or hill crests
- risks arising from the position or movement of other road users
- problems arising from variations in the road surface, weather conditions and visibility.

At the end of your next journey, look back over the way you approached and negotiated hazards and ask yourself the following questions.

Did you always know what was happening behind before changing direction or speed? Did you always have the right position, speed and gear for the hazard?

Were you able to negotiate all the hazards smoothly without any snatched last-minute adjustments?

Did you always give yourself time to react?

How good are you at identifying situations that are potentially dangerous? Next time you ride along a route you use regularly – say your normal route to work – examine the route carefully for situations that are potentially dangerous and where in the past you have not used sufficient caution. Plan how you could negotiate each of these situations in future.

The system of motorcycle control

The system promotes careful observation, early anticipation and planning, and a systematic use of the controls to achieve maximum machine stability. It is a systematic way of dealing with an unpredictable environment. It is central to *Motorcycle Roadcraft*, drawing together all other riding skills in a co-ordinated response to road and traffic conditions. It gives you the time to select the best position, speed and gear to negotiate the hazards safely and efficiently.

Hazards come singly and in clusters; they overlap and change all the time. The system accommodates this continual fluctuation by means of a centrally flexible element – you, the rider. As with the other skills in *Motorcycle Roadcraft*, you have responsibility for using the system actively and intelligently. When you use the system to approach and negotiate a hazard, you consider and use a logical sequence of actions to take you past it safely and efficiently. If new hazards arise, you adapt by reassessing the situation and reapplying the system at an appropriate phase.

The five phases of the system

The system is divided into five phases:

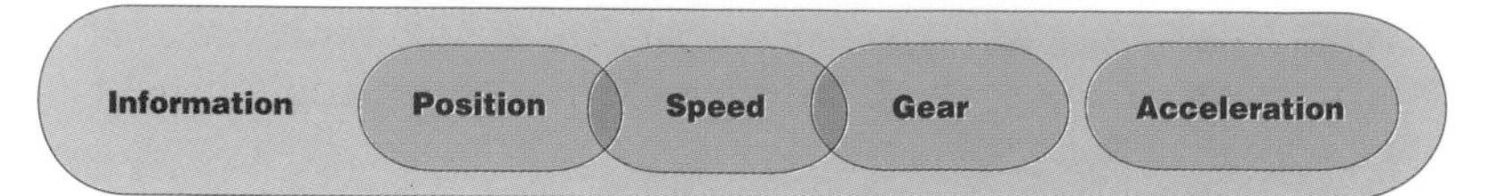

Each phase is dependent on the one before, and you should consider the phases in sequence. Normally you would start by considering your information needs, and then work through each phase in turn. But if road conditions change, you need to consider new information and re-enter the system at an appropriate phase, continuing through it in sequence. The system must be used flexibly in response to actual road conditions; do not follow the sequence rigidly if it is inappropriate to the circumstances.

The phases of the system cover all the points you need to consider on the approach to a hazard. At each phase there are a number of points to consider, but you should only apply those points that are relevant to the situation.

The importance of the information phase

Taking, using and giving information introduces the system, and continues throughout it. You always need to be seeking information to plan your riding and you should provide information whenever other road users could benefit from it. Because of your increased vulnerability as a motorcyclist, your safety and at times your survival depend on your ability to take, use and give information. Information allows you to adapt the system to changes in road circumstances, and so continuous assessment of information overlaps with and runs through all the other phases of the system. It is the framework on which the other phases – position, speed, gear, acceleration – depend.

Information phase: **T** take **U** use **G** give

Continuous assessment of information runs through every phase of the system.

Rear observation and signals

Constantly assess the situation ahead and to the side for changes in the circumstances. Use rear observation (mirror and/or looking behind) as often as is necessary to be fully aware of what is happening behind you. Give a signal whenever it could benefit another road user.

At certain points in the system specific checks for information are important. **Before you change position or speed you need to know what is happening in front, to the sides and behind you; mirror checks/looking behind at these points are essential.** Remember the standard advice for manoeuvring: rear observation – signal – manoeuvre, even though you may at times decide a signal is not necessary.

See Chapter 3, Observation, page 44, Improving your observation skills.

Use of the horn

Sound your horn whenever you think another road user could hear and benefit from it. The purpose of the horn is to inform others that you are there. It gives you no right to proceed, and should never be used as a rebuke. It can be used at any stage of the system. Always be prepared to react to another road user's horn warning.

See Chapter 6, Signals.

The lifesaver check

The lifesaver is a last check over the shoulder into the blind spots to make sure nothing unexpected is happening before committing yourself to a manoeuvre. If you are turning, use it to check the blind spot on the side to which you intend to turn. The place for the lifesaver is just before the first part of the acceleration phase. Use your judgement about when to use it: in congested urban situations a lifesaver check is normally essential, especially when turning right into a minor road, but during high speed overtaking, when you are certain what is happening behind, it is often safer to keep your eyes on what is happening ahead.

When you use a lifesaver, do it early enough to allow you to adopt an alternative plan. There is no use in looking over your shoulder as you start to turn the machine.

The system of motorcycle control

The phases of the system are set out on this page. The diagram explains the key features of the system, and includes cross references to other chapters. These cross references are necessary for a complete understanding of the system, and need to be read in conjunction with it. Other chapters give a full treatment of the different skills called on when you use the system. When and how you read them depends on your own study plan. If you are using *Motorcycle Roadcraft* as part of a course, ask your instructor for advice.

Information

The information phase overlaps every other phase of the system.

Take information
Look all round you. Scan to the front and sides. Carry out rear observation at the appropriate points in the system. Always consider rear observation before you change direction or speed. As you approach, closely observe the quality of the road surface up to and through the hazard.

See Chapter 3, ***Observation****.*

Use information
Using the information you have gathered, plan how to deal with the identified hazards and make contingency plans for dealing with the unexpected. Decide on your next action using the system as a guide. If new hazards arise consider whether you need to re-run the system from an earlier phase.

See Chapter 3, ***Observation****, page 40,* ***Planning****.*

Give information
If you have decided a signal could help other road users, give it; remember other road users include pedestrians and cyclists. Your options include indicators, brakelight, flashing your headlight, arm signals and sounding your horn. Give a signal whenever it could benefit other road users, no matter what stage of the system you are at. Generally the earlier the warning the greater the benefit.

See Chapter 6, ***Signals****.*

Position

Position yourself so that you can negotiate the hazard/s safely and smoothly. Before you change position consider rear observation.

See Chapter 7, ***Positioning****.*

Take account of the road surface and other road users – including pedestrians, cyclists and children.

Continuous

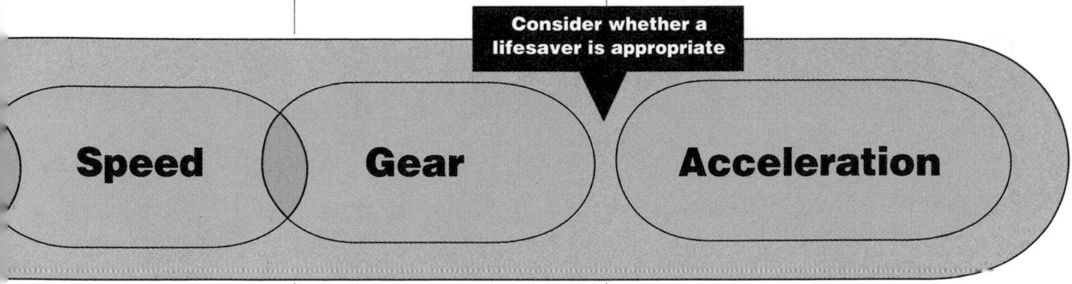

Consider whether a lifesaver is appropriate

Speed

Adjust your speed to that appropriate for the hazard, taking into account visibility, the road surface, the degree of cornering required, the activities of other road users and the possibility of unseen hazards. Use the throttle, brake or (when on slippery surfaces *See* ***Avoiding skids*** *page 99*) gears to give you the speed which will enable you to complete the manoeuvre. During the later stages of braking change to the appropriate gear. Make good use of acceleration sense.

Aim to make all adjustments in speed smoothly and steadily; early anticipation is essential for this.

See Chapter 4, ***Acceleration, using gears and braking,*** *and Chapter 10,* ***Speed and safety****.*

Gear

Select the appropriate gear for the speed at which you intend to negotiate the hazard.

Pass through intermediate gears during the later stages of any braking by the block changing method or by systematically working through the gears, engaging each appropriate gear as speed is lost. Except in slippery conditions, avoid using your gears as brakes. Always avoid late braking and snatched gear changes.

See Chapter 4, ***Acceleration, using gears and braking****.*

Acceleration

Consider rear observation.

Use the throttle to maintain your speed and stability through the hazard. Open the throttle sufficiently to offset any loss of speed due to cornering forces.

Taking account of your speed, the road surface, the amount of turn required, other road users, and the road and traffic conditions ahead and behind, decide whether it is appropriate to accelerate away from the hazard.

Choose an appropriate point to accelerate safely and smoothly, adjust the amount of acceleration to the circumstances.

See Chapter 4, ***Acceleration, using gears and braking*** *and Chapter 5,* ***Cornering, balance and avoiding skids.***

assessment of information runs through every phase of the system.

Use the system flexibly

The key point to remember is that the system depends on your using it intelligently and responsively. It is not an automatic mechanism but has to be adapted by you to the circumstances that arise. Used intelligently, it provides a logical but flexible sequence for dealing with hazards:

- you should consider all the phases of the system on the approach to every hazard, but you may not need to use every phase in a particular situation
- the information phase spans the whole system and entails a constant reassessment of plans
- if a new hazard arises consider whether you need to return to an earlier phase of the system.

See Chapter 3, ***Observation****, page 40,* ***Planning****.*

Once you have learnt the system, practise it continually. It will become second nature, forming the basis upon which the finer points of your riding can be built.

We shall now look at how the system is applied to three of the commonest hazards: a right-hand turn, a left-hand turn and a roundabout.

Practise applying the system

Familiarise yourself with the five phases of the system and practise working through them whenever you ride. Remember to use the system flexibly according to the circumstances.

At first it might help to name each phase out loud as you enter it.

Review your performance and identify whether you:

- consider each phase
- consider all the aspects of each phase
- systematically work through the phases.

Where you have identified problems, work through them one by one, solving the first problem before you go on to the next.

Applying the system to a right-hand turn

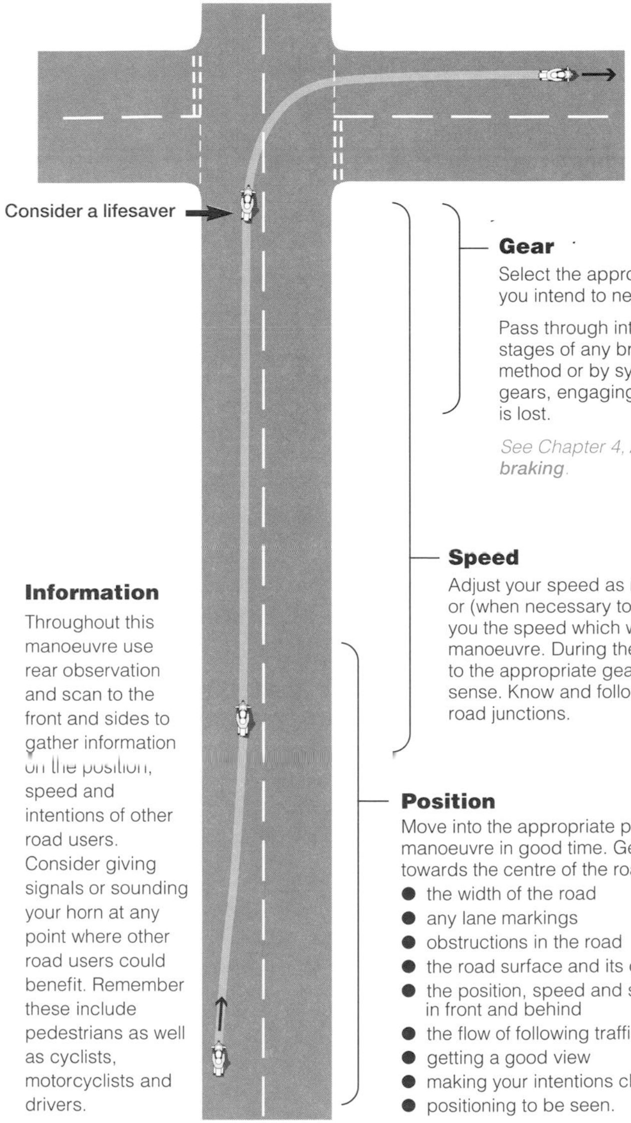

Acceleration

Use the throttle to maintain your speed and stability through the hazard. Open the throttle sufficiently to offset any loss of speed due to cornering forces.

After you start to return to the upright position, choose an appropriate point to accelerate smoothly away from the hazard. Take into account your speed, the road surface, the amount of turn required, other road users, and the road and traffic conditions ahead and behind.

Consider a lifesaver

Gear

Select the appropriate gear for the speed at which you intend to negotiate the hazard.

Pass through intermediate gears during the later stages of any braking by the block changing method or by systematically working through the gears, engaging each appropriate gear as speed is lost.

See Chapter 4, ***Acceleration, using gears and braking***.

Speed

Adjust your speed as necessary. Use the throttle, brake or (when necessary to avoid skidding) gears to give you the speed which will enable you to complete the manoeuvre. During the later stages of braking change to the appropriate gear. Make good use of acceleration sense. Know and follow the *Highway Code* advice on road junctions.

Information

Throughout this manoeuvre use rear observation and scan to the front and sides to gather information on the position, speed and intentions of other road users. Consider giving signals or sounding your horn at any point where other road users could benefit. Remember these include pedestrians as well as cyclists, motorcyclists and drivers.

Position

Move into the appropriate position to make the manoeuvre in good time. Generally this will be towards the centre of the road, but pay attention to:

- the width of the road
- any lane markings
- obstructions in the road
- the road surface and its condition
- the position, speed and size of other traffic – both in front and behind
- the flow of following traffic
- getting a good view
- making your intentions clear to other road users
- positioning to be seen.

Applying the system to a left-hand turn

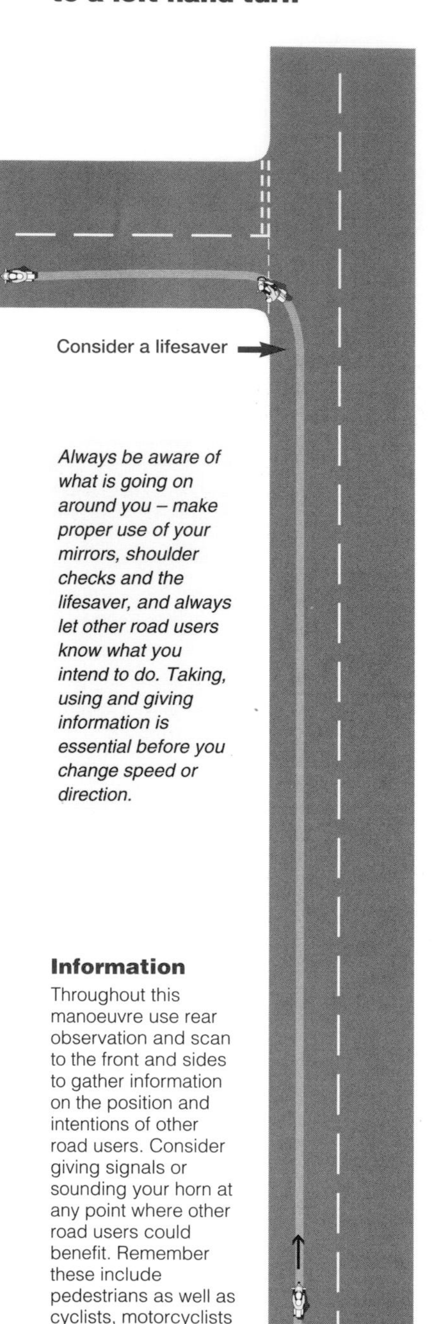

Always be aware of what is going on around you – make proper use of your mirrors, shoulder checks and the lifesaver, and always let other road users know what you intend to do. Taking, using and giving information is essential before you change speed or direction.

Information

Throughout this manoeuvre use rear observation and scan to the front and sides to gather information on the position and intentions of other road users. Consider giving signals or sounding your horn at any point where other road users could benefit. Remember these include pedestrians as well as cyclists, motorcyclists and drivers.

Acceleration

Be aware of the possibility of cyclists and motorbikes moving up quickly on your inside.

Use the throttle to maintain your speed and stability through the hazard. Open the throttle sufficiently to offset any loss of speed due to cornering forces.

Taking account of your speed, the road surface, the amount of turn required, other road users, and the road and traffic conditions ahead and behind, decide whether it is appropriate to accelerate away from the hazard.

Choose an appropriate point to accelerate safely and smoothly, adjust the amount of acceleration to the circumstances. Do not increase speed before you start to return to the upright position.

See Chapter 4, ***Acceleration, using gears and braking****, page 69,* ***Accelerating on bends****.*

Gear

Select the appropriate gear for the speed at which you intend to negotiate the hazard.

Speed

Adjust your speed as necessary. Use the throttle, brake or (when necessary to avoid skidding) gears to give you the speed which will enable you to complete the manoeuvre. During the later stages of braking change to the appropriate gear. Make good use of acceleration sense.

Generally a left turn is slower than a right because the turning arc is tighter. Avoid running wide as you enter the junction or you may come into conflict with other traffic.

Position

Position towards the left of the road but pay attention to:

- the width of the road
- any lane markings
- obstructions in the road
- the road surface and its condition
- the position, speed and size of other traffic – both in front and behind
- the flow of following traffic
- getting a good view
- making your intentions clear to other road users
- positioning to be seen.

Applying the system to approaching a roundabout

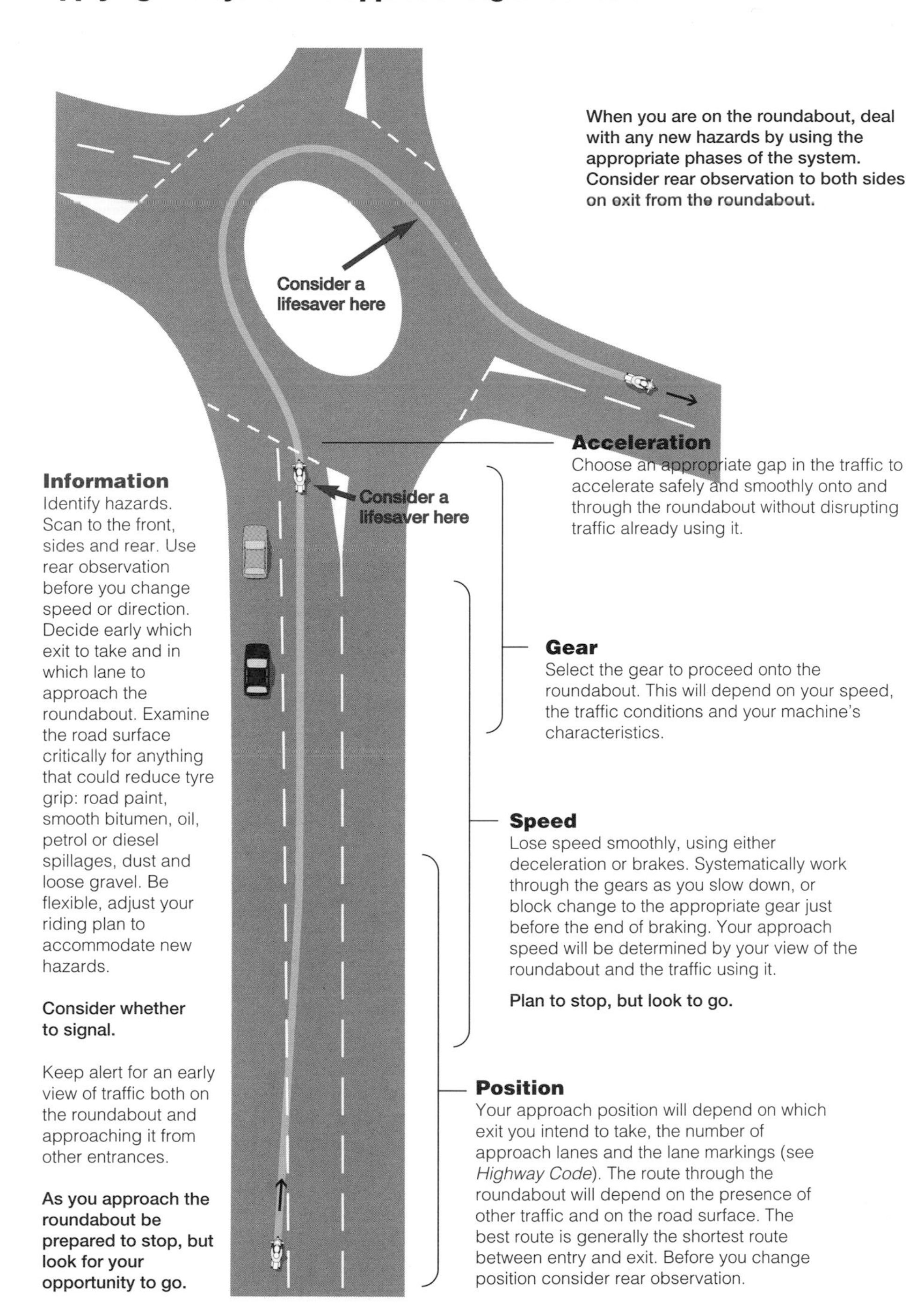

Review

In this chapter we have looked at:

- how a systematic approach to hazards can improve your riding
- different types of hazards
- what the system of motorcycle control is and how to apply it
- the importance of taking, using and giving information
- the importance of rear observation and the lifesaver
- using the system flexibly.

Check your understanding

What causes road accidents?

How does the system of motorcycle control increase the safety of your riding?

What is a hazard, and what are the three main types of hazard that you will meet on the road?

What are the five phases of the system of motorcycle control?

Which phase overlaps and runs through all the other phases?

When should you consider giving a signal?

When should you consider carrying out rear observation?

When should you carry out a lifesaver check?

How should you decide which gear to select?

Why is it vital to use the system flexibly?

Why must you consider road surface conditions before selecting speed, gear, acceleration and curve to negotiate and leave a hazard?

If you have difficulty in answering any of these questions, look back over the relevant part of this chapter to refresh your memory.

Use this chapter to find out:

- why good observation is vital to safe riding
- how to use your observations to make a riding plan
- why a riding plan is important
- how to improve your observation
- how to adapt your riding to speed, weather, road surface and night conditions
- how to make the best use of road signs and markings.

Chapter 3

Observation

Observation

This chapter looks at observation skills and how to apply them to your riding. The first part of the chapter looks at the link between observation and planning. It shows how good planning enables you to make the fullest use of your observation skills and so increase your riding safety. The second part of the chapter looks at observation skills in detail. It highlights important sources of information in the traffic environment and explains techniques for improving your skill at observing and applying this information.

Why you need good observation skills

'Observation' means using sight, hearing and smell to gain as much information about conditions as possible. Keen observation is the foundation of good riding and, for the motorcyclist, can mean the difference between life and death. If you do not know something is there you cannot react to it. Careful observation gives you extra time to think and react, and so gives you more control over your riding.

You may occasionally have caught yourself going along absent-mindedly, with your mind anywhere but on your riding. You are thinking about the incident you are riding to, your job or something else, and only noticing what is happening immediately in front of you. In this state you are highly vulnerable, you are unprepared to deal with a sudden emergency and may well become the victim of other road users' actions. You may also be a source of danger yourself because you are unaware of what other road users are doing.

The *Motorcycle Roadcraft* method of riding requires your active attention to your riding all the time. Your ability to take, use and give information and to apply the system of motorcycle control depends on your skills of observation and planning.

If you normally wear glasses, wear them under your visor when riding. Do not wear tinted glasses at night.

Planning

Safe and effective riding depends on using the information gained from observation to plan your riding actions.

Use the information gained by observation to form a riding plan:

- anticipate hazards
- order hazards in importance
- decide what to do.

The purpose of the plan is to put you in the right position, at the right speed, in the right gear, at the right time to negotiate hazards safely and efficiently. As soon as conditions change a new riding plan is required. Effective planning is a continual process of forming and re-forming plans. Make full use of the opportunities for observation and manoeuvrability available to you as a rider.

The diagram on this page shows how the three stages of planning encourage you to interpret and act on your observations:

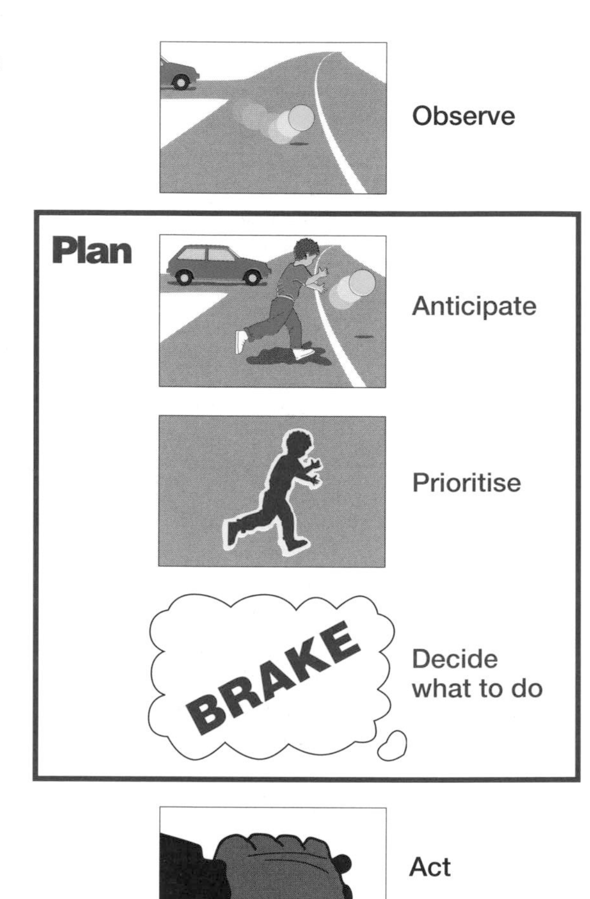

We will now look in more detail at the three stages of planning.

Anticipate

The more time you have to react to a hazard, the more likely you are to deal with it safely. Anticipating hazards gives you extra time. Your ability to anticipate depends on your training, your experience and the amount of effort you put in to developing it. A useful technique to help you develop this ability is commenting aloud (making a running commentary as you ride along on what you are observing and how you plan to deal with it).

Start with what you observe and then use your general riding experience to predict how the situation is likely to unfold: for example, your view ahead will often be obscured by vehicles or the layout of the road, yet you know from experience that hazards may be present in the unseen areas. (See the section on observation links at the end of this chapter.) Search the road for clues which might give you added insight into likely developments. To anticipate means to extract the fullest meaning from your observations. For example, when you see a ball bounce into the road you know there is a good chance that children will run after it.

Anticipating the actions of other road users is important for your own and others' safety. It is unsafe to assume that other road users have either seen you or will react correctly in any given situation. Observing someone's general progress and road behaviour will give you some idea of what sort of driver they are, but even the most conscientious drivers can make mistakes. Carefully observing other drivers' eye, hand and head movements will give you a better idea of their intentions, but you should always give yourself a safety margin of extra time and space to allow for others' mistakes. If you have a serious accident, being in the right is small consolation.

*Skilful riders **anticipate** in order to make their plans more effective.*

Order hazards in importance

Among the many observed or anticipated hazards that you identify, you must decide which are significant, and which is the most important. Grade the risks, and deal with them in order of importance. The importance of a hazard may change rapidly, and you must be ready to change your priorities accordingly.

The intensity of danger associated with hazards varies with:

- the hazard itself
- how close it is to you
- road layout and road surface conditions
- whether the hazard is stationary or moving, and if so, its direction
- how fast you are approaching it.

The greater the element of danger, the higher the priority that you should give it.

See Chapter 2, The system of motorcycle control.

Decide what to do

When you have ranked the observed and anticipated hazards in order of importance, you are in a position to decide on your course of action. The aim of your plan is to ensure the safety of yourself and other road users at all times. The appropriate course of action takes account of:

- what can be seen
- what cannot be seen
- what might reasonably be expected to happen
- which hazards represent the greatest threat
- what to do if things turn out differently from expected (contingency plans).

Generally things do not just happen, they take a while to develop – good planning depends on early observation and early anticipation of risk.

If you plan your riding you should be able to make decisions in a methodical way at any moment and without hesitation. While you are riding you should be continuously anticipating, ranking hazards in importance and deciding what to do. At first you might find it difficult to consciously work through these three stages all the time, but with practice this will become second nature and prove a quick and reliable guide to action.

Throughout your next journey, aim to apply the three stages of planning:

- anticipate
- rank hazards in importance
- decide what to do.

During your journey monitor your performance. How successful are you at planning? On how many occasions are you simply reacting to events rather than anticipating them?

Grading a hazard in terms of risk

The chart below shows five different risk situations.

	Risk scale	Your action
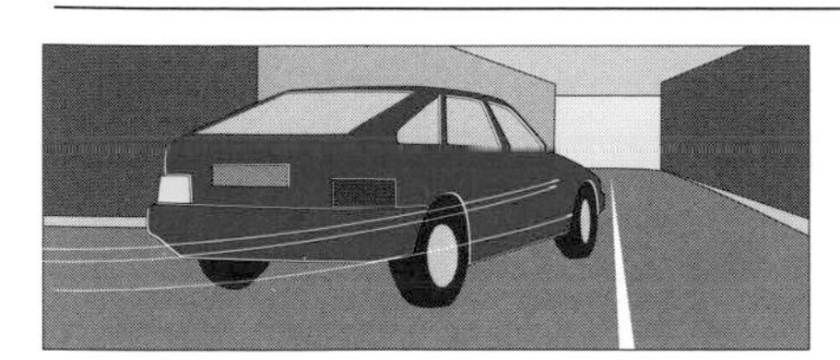	**1** A car pulls out at a junction, turning left and joining your path.	Here the risk is a positive danger requiring drastic action to avoid a collision. Brake hard and move out if possible. No time to sound the horn – in fact the use of the horn may be counter-productive. The driver of the car may brake.
	**2** A car is stationary at the junction and angled to turn left. The driver has not looked in your direction. The brake lights go off and the car begins to move.	This situation contains serious risk. Alter your position if you have not already done so and lose speed sharply. Make a long horn note.
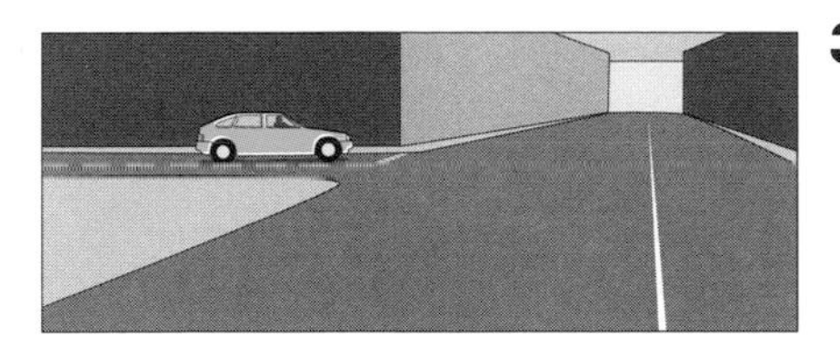	**3** A car is on its final approach to the junction, slowing as if to stop, but you do not have eye contact with the driver.	The driver of the car is unaware of your presence. The risk is a real one. The driver may pull out. Alter your course to maximise the distance between you and the other car, and alter your speed. Consider a short horn note.
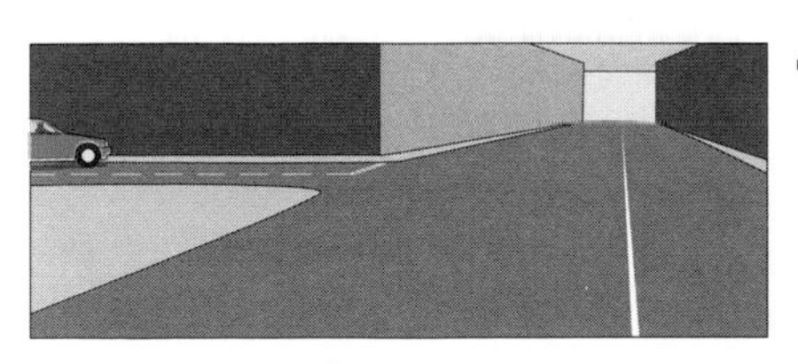	**4** A car comes into view approaching the junction from the left.	The presence of the car represents a slight risk. Consider altering your position and speed.
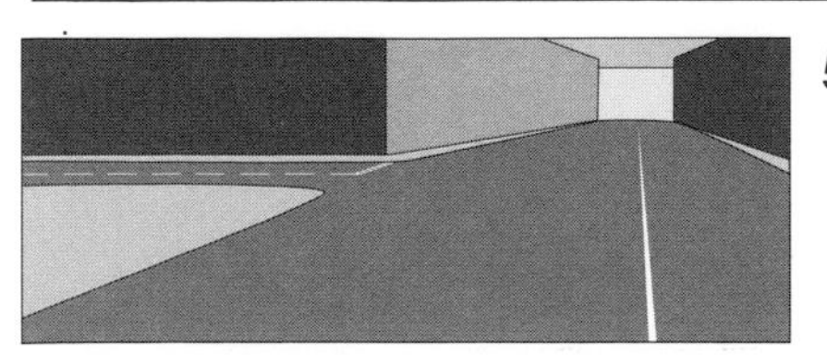	**5** Road junction is free of traffic.	Every road junction poses a risk. This junction is clear and vision is good. No action is required other than to keep making vision scans until the potential risk passes.

Improving your observation skills

We shall now look at ways of developing observational skills.

Observational advantages of a motorcycle

Motorcyclists have observational advantages over most car drivers. The rider sits higher and has greater flexibility in positioning the machine to get the best view. You should be aware of these advantages and use them to the full, although you should never sacrifice safety for a better view.

Use your eyes – scanning

Use your eyes to build up a picture of what is happening all around you, as far as you can see, in every direction. The best way to build this picture is to use your eyes in a scanning motion which sweeps the whole environment: the distance, the mid-ground, the foreground, the sides and rear. Riders who scan the environment looking for different kinds of hazard have a lower risk of accidents than riders who concentrate only on one area, so develop the habit of scanning repeatedly and regularly.

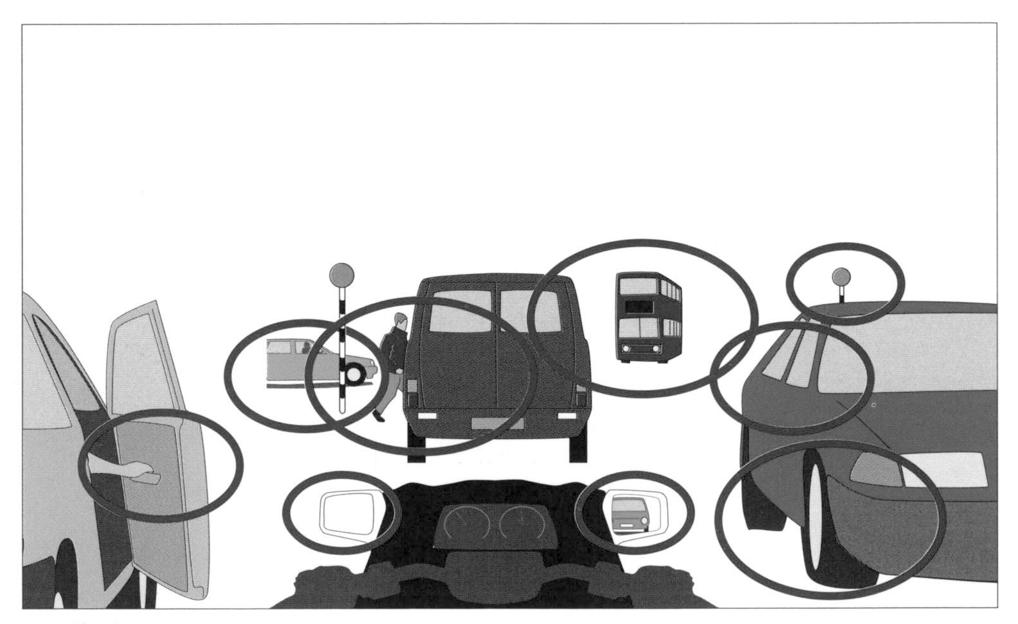

Routine scanning enables you to spot all areas of risk, which you should then check and re-check.

Scanning is a continuous process. When a new view opens out in front of you, scan the scene. By scanning the whole of the environment you will know where the areas of risk are. Check and recheck these risk areas in your visual sweeps. Avoid staring at particular risk areas because this stops you placing them in the broader context. Use your mirrors frequently, and consider checking over your shoulder when it is not safe to rely on your mirrors alone – for example, when moving off from the kerb, turning into a junction, joining a motorway, changing lanes or leaving a roundabout.

Rear observation

Rear observation refers to a combination of mirror checks and looking behind which ensures you are always fully aware of what is happening behind you. Looking behind is important because the view through the mirrors on some motorcycles is restricted, leaving significant blind spots. You need to look into these blind spots to make sure you know what is happening there.

Looking behind covers a range of head movements from a quick glance to the side to a full backwards twist of the head. Which you use depends on the circumstances, but the purpose is the same in all cases – to make sure that your intended course and speed will safeguard you from collision.

Use judgement in deciding when to look behind. Obviously when you are looking behind you are not looking ahead. This could be hazardous if, for example, you are close to the vehicle in front or if you are overtaking at speed. Equally there are situations when it is dangerous not to look behind, such as a right turn into a minor road.

Because there is an element of risk in taking your eyes off the road ahead, avoid prolonged rear observation or making two rear observations when one is sufficient.

See Chapter 2, *The system of motorcycle control*, page 31, *The lifesaver check*.

Consider rear observation when you are about to change position or speed as you approach and negotiate a hazard. The system of motorcycle control advises when to do lifesaver checks.

Peripheral vision

Peripheral vision is the area of eyesight surrounding the central area of sharply defined vision. Learn to react to your peripheral vision as well as your central vision. The eye's receptors in this area are different from the central receptors, and are particularly good at sensing movement. This helps to alert us to areas that need to be examined more closely. Peripheral vision gives us our sense of speed and lateral position, registers the movement of other road users and acts as a cue for central vision. It is the first area of sight to diminish as we grow tired.

How helmets and visors affect observation

Your helmet and/or visor may restrict your peripheral vision. To overcome this, move your head slightly from side to side so that you are aware of what is happening alongside you.

It is important to keep your visor and spectacles free from water droplets, mist or scratches. In wet, misty or cold weather use anti-mist/anti-water sprays or compounds on both surfaces of your visor and spectacles. Keep the lenses clean and protect them from scratches. If the lenses do become scratched replace them.

Tinted lenses reduce vision at night and in conditions of poor visibility.

Compare your peripheral vision when wearing your safety helmet and when it is removed. If your helmet restricts your vision remember to compensate by regularly moving your head to be aware of what is happening alongside you.

How speed affects observation

At 70 mph the shortest distance in which you can react and stop is 96 metres (315 feet). This is approximately the distance between motorway marker posts (100 metres). To anticipate events at this speed you need to be scanning everything between your machine and the horizon.

- At speed, vibration can distort vision.
- The faster you go the further you need to look ahead. As your speed increases, consciously look beyond the point where your eyes naturally come to rest so as to allow yourself sufficient time to react.
- Fatigue limits your ability to see. When you are tired slow down and take a rest.
- Speed increases the distance you travel before you can react to what you have seen. You need to build this into your safe stopping distance. When you double your speed you quadruple your braking distance.

- Your ability to take in foreground detail decreases with speed and increases as you slow down. In areas of high traffic density such as town centres, you must slow down to be able to take in all the information necessary to ride safely.

Adjust your speed according to how well you can see, the complexity of the situation and the distance it will take you to stop. You must always be able to stop within the distance you can see to be clear.

Zones of visibility

The road around you is made up of different zones of visibility. In some areas your view will be good and in others you will only be able to see what is immediately in front of you. Where your view is restricted, use alternative sources of information, making the most of any glimpses of wider views that you can get. Typical areas with restricted views are junctions in towns and winding lanes in the country.

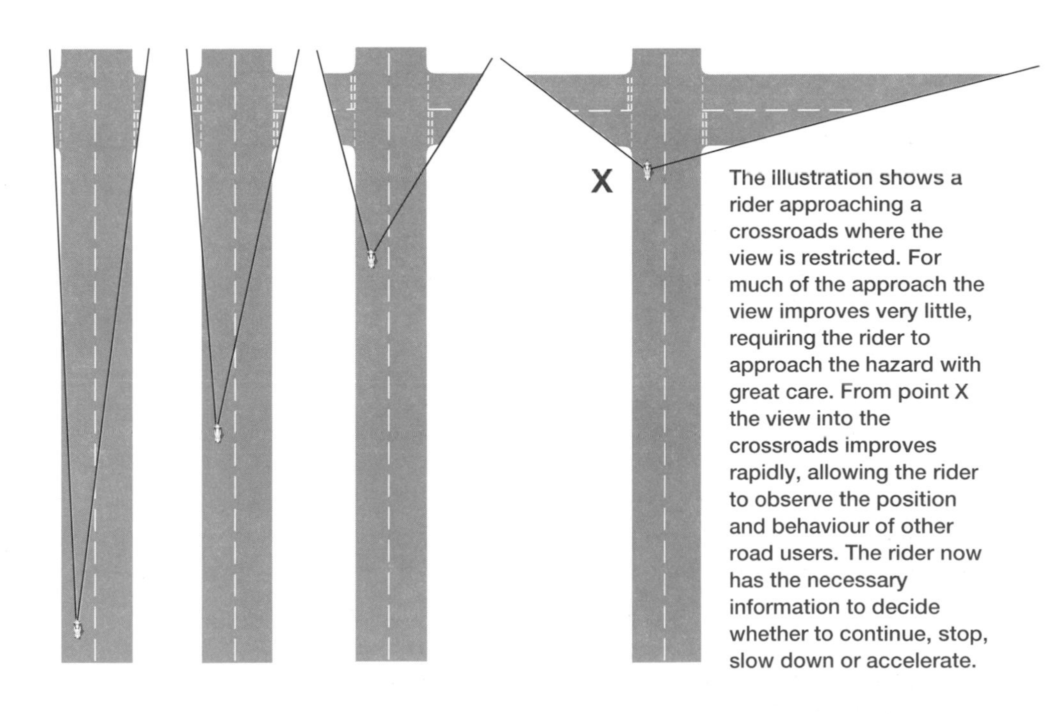

The illustration shows a rider approaching a crossroads where the view is restricted. For much of the approach the view improves very little, requiring the rider to approach the hazard with great care. From point X the view into the crossroads improves rapidly, allowing the rider to observe the position and behaviour of other road users. The rider now has the necessary information to decide whether to continue, stop, slow down or accelerate.

When you approach a hazard where your view is restricted, position your bike to get the best view that is consistent with safety. Take every opportunity, however brief, to improve your observation of converging roads and the road ahead. Opportunities are presented by open spaces and breaks in hedges, fences or walls. It is often possible to assess the severity of a bend or gradient by the position of trees, hedges or lamp posts. Look for these features:

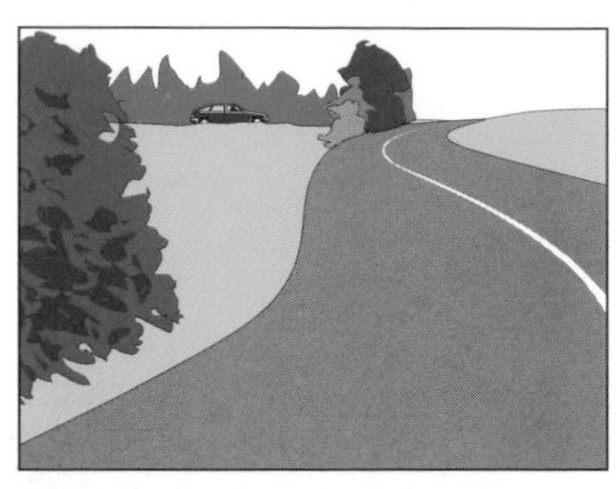

open spaces and breaks in hedges, fences and walls on the approach to a blind junction

the curvature of a row of lamp posts or trees

reflections in shop windows

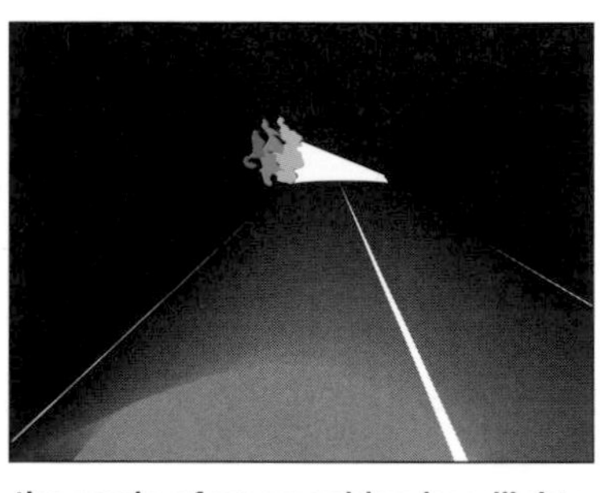

the angle of approaching headlights

Next time you ride along a familiar route, make a mental note of the opportunities to use additional sources of information.

moving shadow or light cast by low sunlight or headlights.

Keep your distance

Other vehicles also affect how much you can see. The closer you are to the vehicle in front the less you will be able to see beyond it, especially if it is large. In slow-moving traffic adopt the best viewing position and drop back slightly so that you can see what is happening two or three vehicles in front.

When you are following a large lorry you will need to keep well back and take views to both sides of the vehicle.

It is vital to have a good view of the road ahead because of the speeds involved. Your view will depend on the curvature and gradient of the carriageway, the lane that you are in, the size and position of other vehicles and your viewing height. Allowing for these, you should keep back far enough from the vehicle in front to maintain a safe following distance. Avoid sitting in the blind spot of other vehicles by overtaking briskly or dropping back. Do a shoulder check to make sure that no one is sitting in your own blind spot before you change lanes.

> Do you know exactly where the offside and nearside central blind spots are on the machines you ride? When you have a safe opportunity sit in your normal riding position on the stationary bike and look through the mirrors. Identify the areas to the nearside and the offside that you cannot see through them. Turn your head over your right shoulder until you can see into the blind spots to the right and behind you. Then turn your head over your left shoulder until you can see into the blind spots to the left and behind you. Remember the importance of shoulder checks.

How well do you observe and plan?

Now would be a good time to check whether you actively observe and plan your riding. Next time you ride over an unfamiliar route, run through these questions before and after your journey to identify your strengths and weaknesses.

Do you constantly observe what is happening:

in the distance?

in the mid-ground?

in front of you?

each side of you?

behind you?

Do you anticipate what is likely to happen and adapt your riding accordingly?

Do you rank the hazards you have observed or anticipated in order of importance?

Do you use your observations to plan your actions?

Do you make contingency plans?

Many people relax their concentration when riding along familiar routes, so assess your performance over a familiar route as well.

Keep a record of any weaknesses you identify and repeat these tests at a later date (say in a fortnight) to see how you are progressing.

Weather conditions

The weather affects your physical and mental condition, how far you can see, and how your machine handles. Assessing the weather and anticipating its effects are central to your observation and riding plan. When weather conditions reduce visibility, you should reduce your speed and regularly check your actual speed on the speedometer. Always be able to stop within the distance you can see to be clear.

*See Chapter 1, **Becoming a better rider**, page 23, **Clothing**, and page 19, **Fatigue**.*

Examples of weather conditions which reduce visibility are:

- cold weather
- fog and mist
- heavy rain
- hail
- snow and sleet
- bright sunshine.

Many of these weather conditions cause misting or droplet formation on visors. Use anti-misting sprays on both surfaces and spray the mirrors as well. If misting occurs due to breath, raise your visor slightly to increase the airflow over the inner surface. Keep your visor clean, even if you have to stop to do so. On motorways these problems are often accentuated because of the greater exposure to the weather, the speed and the spray from other vehicles. Windshields should also be kept clean.

See Chapter 1, ***Becoming a better rider****, page 22,* ***Conspicuity****.*

Use of lights in bad weather

Choose your lights according to the circumstances. Lights have two purposes: they help you to see better and they help others to see you. In daylight the second purpose is often the more important.

- Switch on your dipped headlight when visibility is poor in daylight or in fading light. Use a dipped headlight in rain, snow, mist or fog.
- Use a dipped headlight when going from good light into poor, for example when entering an avenue of trees.
- When you leave the fog, switch off your rear foglight so as not to dazzle following drivers.
- Do not use your main headlight beam when you are behind another vehicle in fog – it may dazzle the driver, and will cast a shadow of the vehicle on the fog ahead, disrupting the driver's view.
- Remember that the brilliance of rear foglights masks the brakelights – allow more distance between you and the vehicle in front and aim to brake gently yourself.

Riding in bad weather

If you must make a journey in bad weather, use anti-misting spray on your visor, spectacles, if worn, and mirrors. In fog, rain, or snow regularly check your speedometer for your actual speed. You cannot rely on your eyes to judge speed accurately in these conditions. Low visibility distorts your perception of speed.

Observing when visibility is low

When visibility is low, ride so you can stop in the distance you can see to be clear. Use the edge of the carriageway, marker lines, hazard lines and cat's eyes as a guide, especially when approaching a road junction or corner. Staring into featureless mist tires the eyes very quickly. Focus instead on what you can see: the vehicle in front, the edge of the road or the road ahead. Avoid fixing your focus on the tail lights of the vehicle in front because they will tend to draw you towards it. You could collide if it stopped suddenly. Be ready to use your horn to inform other road users of your presence.

Always be prepared for a sudden stop in the traffic ahead. Do not follow closely, and only overtake other traffic when you can see that it is absolutely safe to do so. This is seldom possible in fog, especially on a two-way road. At junctions when visibility is low listen for other vehicles, and consider using your horn.

Anticipating the effects of wind

Strong winds, especially cross-winds, are hazardous because they can blow you off course. Sudden gusts of cross-wind are probably the most dangerous. These are likely to occur:

- in gusty weather
- when leaving the shelter of buildings and hedges at gateways, junctions and at the end of building/hedge lines
- when passing or being passed by a large vehicle
- in exposed places: bridges, viaducts, hill crests, etc.

When strong winds are likely, keep your speed low and plan your course to give additional space to your downwind side. Even at speeds as low as 30 mph you may be blown about. Larger machines with full fairings and closed-in bodies are particularly at risk of deflection in strong winds.

See Chapter 9, ***Motorway riding****, page 159,* ***High winds****.*

Weather and the road surface

Besides affecting visibility, the weather will also affect the road surface. Snow, rain or ice will greatly reduce the grip of the tyres, making skids and aquaplaning more likely. Standing water, from whatever cause, also reduces tyre grip.

See Chapter 5, ***Cornering, balance and avoiding skids****, page 99,* ***Avoiding skids****.*

Be aware that special hazards exist in summer. Dust on the road reduces tyre grip. Rain may produce a slippery road surface especially after a long dry spell. Other hazards include melted tarmac and loose chippings.

Micro climates

Look out for micro climates which can cause frost and wet patches to linger in some areas after they have disappeared elsewhere. Landscape features such as valley bottoms, shaded hillsides and shaded slopes, or large areas of shadow cast by trees or buildings can cause ice to linger and result in sudden skidding. Bridge surfaces are often colder than the surrounding roads because they are exposed on all sides, and can be icy when nearby roads are not. Patchy fog is particularly dangerous and is a common catalyst for multiple pile-ups. Look out for the features mentioned earlier that promote wind gusting.

Ice and wetness can linger in areas of shadow.

Adapt your riding to the weather conditions

Bad weather is often blamed for causing accidents, but the real cause is inappropriate riding for the conditions that exist. In dense fog, riding at a speed at which you can stop in the distance you can see to be clear means riding so slowly that many trips are not worth while. The best way to deal with a skid is not to get into it in the first place. Careful observation, the correct speed and adequate braking distances are crucial for safe riding but they are especially important in difficult weather conditions. Accidents occur when these rules are ignored.

Road surface

The type and condition of the road surface is critical to riders. Thorough scanning of it and adaptation to what is observed is essential for safe riding. The surface affects tyre grip and machine handling characteristics. Tyre grip is fundamental to riding control because it determines steering, banking, acceleration and braking. Most riders do not pay sufficient attention to this. Always look well ahead to identify changes in the road surface, and adjust your approach speed and the strength of your braking, acceleration, banking and steering to retain adequate road holding.

A thinking rider is always aware of the surroundings and how they might affect the road surface:

- **country roads** – tar-banding (the tar joint around repairs), mud or other deposits, wet leaves in autumn, spilt grain in summer
- **urban roads** – frequent drains and slippery metal covers, tar-banding and surface variation due to service excavations; oil, diesel, petrol spillages and road paint
- **filling/service stations** – large amounts of fuels spilt on roads at bends and nearby roundabouts, especially on or near motorways.

Always observe the camber of the road on a curve or bend. The slope of the camber increases stability if it falls in the direction of lean; it reduces stability if it rises in the direction of lean. If you cross over the crown of the road on a left-hand bend you enter an area where the slope of the camber is destabilising.

See Chapter 5, ***Cornering, balance and avoiding skids****, page 89,* ***Camber and superelevation.***

The surfaces of most roads are good for road holding when they are clean and dry. At hazards such as roundabouts or junctions, tyre deposit and fuel spillage may make the surface slippery at precisely the point where effective steering, braking and acceleration are needed to negotiate the hazard safely.

Surfacing materials	Grip characteristics	Problems
Tarmac or asphalt	Tarmac or asphalt surfaces give a good grip when they are dressed with stones or chips.	In time they become polished and lose some of their skid resistant properties.
Concrete	Concrete road surfaces often have roughened ribs which give a good skid resistant surface.	Some hold water, which freezes in cold weather and creates a slippery surface which is not easily seen.
Cobbles	Low grip when wet.	Rain increases the likelihood of skidding.
Anti-skid surfaces	Good when new, deteriorates with age.	Ageing reduces grip.

Road surface irregularities

Keep a careful look out for irregularities in the road surface. If you can alter your position to avoid them without danger, do so. If you cannot, carry out rear observation and slow down. Where possible ride over them in an upright position. Common surface irregularities are:

Road paint

White plastic paint used in road markings is very slippery when wet. Where possible avoid such markings, or choose a position that will minimise the danger. For example where there is a SLOW marking on the road ride between the letters rather than over them.

Road joints

Take care where road repairs have left poor joints between the reinstated surface and the existing surface. Even slight differences in height can affect machine stability, deflecting the machine from its intended course. Avoid road joints running along the length of the road. Tar-banding provides less grip than the surrounding surfaces, especially when wet.

Metal covers

Manhole covers, drain covers and temporary metal sheeting provide poor grip especially when dusty or wet. Unfortunately manhole covers are often in the natural line of a bike. Avoid them where you can.

Physical defects

Potholes, projecting manhole covers, sunken gullies and general debris are a serious danger to the rider. Keep a careful lookout for them and ride round them if possible. Otherwise brake while you are on the approach and pass over them slowly. Consider rear observation before you brake.

The road surface in winter

In winter, the ice or frost covering on road surfaces is not always uniform. Isolated patches remain iced up when other parts have thawed out, and certain slopes are especially susceptible to this. Be on the lookout for ice or frost patches, which you can detect by their appearance and by the behaviour of other vehicles. Adjust your riding early to avoid skidding.

Riding through water

Riding at speed through water can sharply deflect you from your intended course and cause you to lose control. Extra care is needed at night when it is difficult to distinguish between a wet road surface and flood water. Flood water can gather quickly where the road dips and at the sides of the road in poorly drained low lying areas. Dips often occur under bridges.

As you approach a flooded area you should slow down. Avoid riding through water wherever possible, as water may conceal a deep hole. If possible, use the part of the road that is not flooded. When you have to ride through water, slow down to a walking pace and ride through the shallowest part, which is usually the crown of the road. Be alert to the possibility of hidden obstructions, subsidence or oncoming traffic.

If the road is entirely submerged, stop the machine in a safe place and cautiously find out how deep the water is. The depth of water that you can safely ride through depends on how high your machine stands off the ground and where the electrical components are positioned. If you decide to continue, follow the steps below.

- Engage first gear and keep the engine running fast by slipping the clutch. This prevents water entering the exhaust pipe. Use the rear brake to control the road speed, especially when riding downhill into a ford.
- Ride through the water at a low and constant speed to avoid making a bow wave. Keep the machine upright.
- When you leave the water ride slowly and apply the brakes lightly until they grip. Repeat this again after a short while until you are confident that both brakes are working normally. This also applies if you have pushed your machine through the water.

Night riding

Observing in night conditions (which means anything less than full daylight) is more difficult and yields less information. As the light dwindles your ability to see the road ahead also declines – contrast falls, colours fade and edges become indistinct.

At night your eyes need all the help you can give them. Visors, spectacles, mirrors, windscreens and the lenses of lights and indicators should all be clean to give the best possible visibility. The slightest film of moisture, grease or dirt on visors, spectacles or mirrors will break up light and increase glare, making it harder to distinguish what is going on. Scratches on visors cause starring when struck by the light from other vehicles, which reduces visibility to nil. If droplets form on your visor try tilting your head so the airstream removes them. Do not wear tinted spectacles or visors at night.

See page 46, *How helmets and visors affect observation*.

Lights should be correctly aligned, and adjusted for the machine. The bulbs should all work and the switching equipment should function properly.

Lights

On unlit roads your headlight should be on main beam unless it is dipped because of other road users.

Use a dipped headlight:

- in built-up areas
- in situations where a dipped headlight is more effective than the main beam, for example when going round a left-hand bend or over a hump-back bridge
- in heavy rain, snow and fog when the falling droplets reflect glare from a headlight on full beam.

Dip your headlight to avoid dazzling oncoming drivers, the driver in front or other road users: when you overtake another vehicle, return to full beam when you are parallel with it.

You should always ride so as to be able to stop within the area that you can see to be clear; at night this is the area lit by your headlight unless there is full streetlighting. Even in the best conditions your ability to assess the speed and position of oncoming vehicles is reduced at night, so you need to allow an extra safety margin.

Dazzle

Headlights shining directly into your eyes may dazzle you. This can happen on sharp right-hand bends and steep inclines, and when the lights of oncoming vehicles are undipped or badly adjusted. The intensity of the light bleaches the retina of the eye and the bleaching effect can continue for some moments afterwards. During this time you can see nothing, which is obviously dangerous.

To avoid dazzle, look towards the nearside edge of the road. This enables you to keep to your course but does not tell you what is happening in the road ahead, so slow down or stop if necessary. If you are dazzled by undipped headlights, flash your own light quickly to alert the other driver, but do not retaliate by putting on your full beam. If you did, both you and the other driver would be converging blind. If you suffer temporary blindness, stop and wait until your eyes have adjusted.

Following other vehicles at night

When you follow another vehicle, dip your headlight and allow a sufficient gap so that your light does not dazzle the driver in front. When you overtake, move out early with your headlight still dipped. If a warning is necessary, flash your light instead of using the horn. When you are alongside the other vehicle return to full beam. If you are overtaken, dip your headlight when the overtaking vehicle draws alongside you and keep it dipped until it can be raised without dazzling the other driver.

Information from other vehicles' lights

You can get useful information from the front and rear lights of other vehicles; for example, the sweep of the headlights of vehicles approaching a bend can indicate the sharpness of the bend, and the brakelights of vehicles in front can give you an early warning to reduce speed.

There are other times when intelligent use of information given by lights will help your riding.

Reflective studs and markings

Reflective studs and markings are a good source of information about road layout at night. To get the most out of them you need to be familiar with the *Highway Code*. Roadside marker posts reflect your headlight and show you the direction of a curve before you can see where the actual road goes. Generally red markers are on the nearside and white markers on the offside.

Cat's eyes

Cat's eyes indicate the type of white line along the centre of the road. Generally the more white paint in the line, the greater the number of cat's eyes. They are particularly helpful when it is raining at night and the glare of headlights makes it difficult to see.

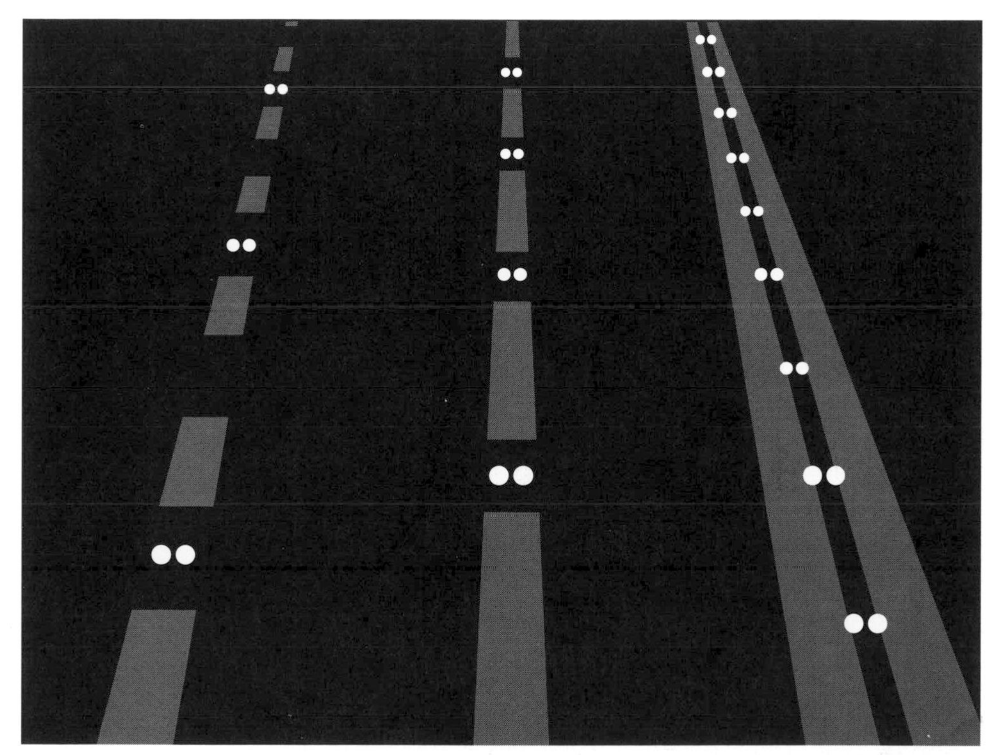

Centre lines: one cat's eye every other gap.

Hazard lines: one cat's eye every gap.

Double white lines: twice as many cat's eyes as hazard lines.

Other ways to improve observation at night

- Keep your speed down when you leave brightly lit areas to allow time for your eyes to adjust to the lower level of lighting.
- Certain types of spectacles – such as those with tinted lenses and those with photochromatic lenses – may be unsuitable for night riding, so check with your optician.

Night fatigue

Night riding is tiring because it puts extra strain on your eyes, and your body naturally wants to slow down as night draws on. Be aware of this problem and take appropriate action to deal with it. If you are having difficulty keeping your eyes open, you are a danger to yourself and other road users; find somewhere safe to stop, and rest until you are alert enough to continue safely. Allow for more stops on a long journey at night to allow for the additional fatigue.

*See Chapter 1, **Becoming a better rider**, page 19, **Fatigue** for further advice.*

Road signs and markings

Road signs and markings provide warnings about approaching hazards, and instructions and information about road use. They need to be incorporated into your riding plan as early as possible. To make the best possible use of road signs and markings you should follow the steps below.

- Observe – actively search for road signs and markings in your observation scans, and incorporate the information they give you into your riding plan. Many drivers and riders fail to see and make use of them, and so lose valuable information.
- Understand – be able to recognise them immediately. You should be familiar with the current edition of the *Highway Code* and the *Know your Traffic Signs* book. Everyone's memory declines over time, so check your recall of road signs and markings on a regular basis.
- React – react to a sign or marking by looking ahead to what it refers to and building the information into your riding plan. Where the sign or marking refers to an unseen hazard, anticipate the hazard and adapt your plan accordingly.

The more road paint the greater the danger

Sometimes you will see several road signs on the same pole. These should generally be read from top to bottom. The nearest event is shown by the top sign, the next nearest event by the sign below that, and so on. Always use your own observations to link the signs to the road layout ahead.

Unofficial road signs

Make use of unofficial road signs such as 'Mud on Road', 'Car Boot Sale' and 'Concealed Entrance'. They provide additional information and help you anticipate the road conditions ahead.

Do you always build information from road signs into your riding plan?

When was the last time you looked at road signs in the current *Highway Code*?

Next time you ride, test your observation skills by seeing if you can correctly predict hazards and the road signs warning of them before you actually see the signs.

Local road knowledge

Increasing your local knowledge of the roads can help your riding. Town riding puts heavy demands on your observation, reactions and riding skills, and you need to be alert at all times. At complicated junctions, where it is important to get into the correct lane, local knowledge is a valuable aid. But even when you know the layout of main road junctions, one-way streets, roundabouts and other local features, always plan on the basis of what you can *actually see* – not what usually happens. Inattentiveness is a major cause of accidents and riders are least attentive on roads they know well. Nine out of ten accidents occur on roads that the rider is familiar with.

Making observation links

Observation links are clues to the likely behaviour of other road users. You should constantly aim to build up your own stock of observation links which will help you anticipate road and traffic conditions. Here are some examples.

When you see...	**Look out for...**
A cluster of lamp posts 	Probable roundabout ahead. Anticipate fuel spillages.
A single lamp post on its own 	The exit point of a junction. Anticipate fuel spillages and vehicles emerging.
No gap in a bank of trees ahead 	Road curves to left or right.
Rainbow patterns on a wet road or smell of petroleum products	Diesel, petrol or oil spilt on the road surface.
Railway line beside road	Road will often go over or under it, often with sharp turns.

When you see...	Look out for...
A pedestrian calls a cab	Cab stopping suddenly or turning or moving away from rank. Pedestrian stepping into the road.
A row of parked vehicles	Doors opening, vehicles moving off. Pedestrians stepping out from behind vehicles. Small children hidden from view.
Ice-cream vans, mobile shops, school buses, etc	Pedestrians, especially children.
A bus at a stop	Pedestrians crossing the road to and from the bus. Bus moving off, possibly at an angle.
Pedal cyclists	Inexperienced cyclist doing something erratic. Cyclist looking over shoulder with the intention of turning right. Strong winds causing wobble. Young cyclist doing something dangerous.
Fresh mud or other deposits on road. Newly mown grass, etc	Slow moving vehicles or animals just around the bend.
Post office vans, trades vehicles, etc	Points where the vehicle may stop, eg post box, shops, public houses, garages, building sites, etc.
Pull-ins, petrol stations, pubs, parking places, etc	Vehicles moving in and out, anticipate fuel spillages.
Motorway access points	Vehicles in nearside lane moving out.
Accident	Others slowing down to look.

Write down some of your own observation links in the space provided below.

When you see...	Look out for...

Review

In this chapter we have looked at:

- observation skills that will help to improve your riding
- the link between observation, planning and acting, and the need to anticipate and order hazards in importance
- scanning and using peripheral vision to get the maximum information from observation
- rear observation
- how helmets and visors affect observation
- how speed affects your vision
- using additional sources of information when your view is restricted
- weather conditions to watch out for and how to adjust your riding to poor visibility
- ways of improving observation when you are riding at night
- making full use of information from road signs and markings
- increasing your skill at making observation links.

Check your understanding

What is the purpose of a riding plan?

What are the three key stages of planning?

How do you use your eyes to get the maximum information about your riding environment?

How can you get more information when your view is restricted?

In what ways does speed affect your vision?

What are the weather conditions that reduce visibility?

When should you switch your dipped headlight on?

Which visors should you not wear at night?

What hazards should you look out for on the road surface?

What are the three steps for building road signs and markings into your riding plan?

Describe at least three examples of observation links.

If you have difficulty in answering any of these questions, look back over the relevant part of this chapter to refresh your memory.

Use this chapter to find out more about:

- tyre grip
- machine balance
- accelerating
- using the gears
- braking.

Chapter 4

Accelerating, using gears and braking

Developing your skill at controlling your machine

The aim of this chapter is to increase your control of your machine. Together with the chapter on cornering, it aims to give you complete control over moving, stopping and changing the direction of your machine at all times. To achieve this level of skill you need a good understanding of the controls and how they relate to each other. This chapter looks in detail at the throttle, gears, brakes and at how to make best use of them.

Although we discuss the controls individually, it is important to understand that in use they are closely inter-related with each other and with cornering. They depend for their effectiveness on the grip between the tyres and the road. Because of this, cornering is included in the discussion of tyre grip. There is a full explanation of cornering in the next chapter.

Control of your machine is totally dependent on the grip between the tyres and the road surface.

The tyre grip trade-off

Your ability to control your machine, and the safety of yourself and other road users, depends on the tyre grip available. In any given situation there is a limited amount of tyre grip and this is shared between accelerating, braking and cornering forces. If more tyre grip is used for braking or accelerating, there is less available for cornering, and vice versa.

Tyre grip is not necessarily the same on each wheel. It varies with the load on the wheel and this affects the machine's balance and how it handles. Braking, changing direction and accelerating each alter the distribution of the load.

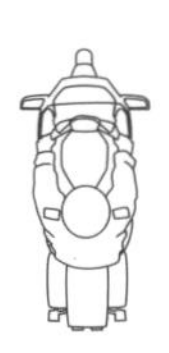

Steady speed weight is evenly distributed

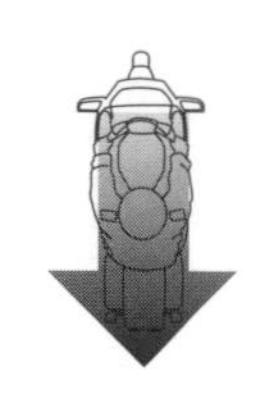

Accelerating weight shifts to the back

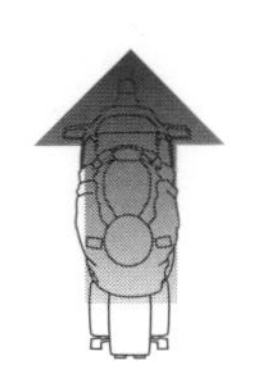

Braking weight shifts to the front

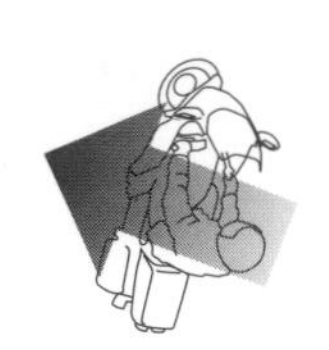

Cornering weight shifts to the outside of the curve, rider counterbalances by banking

Cornering and accelerating weight shifts to the outside of the curve (counter-balanced by banking) and to the back

Cornering and braking weight shifts to the outside of the curve (counter-balanced by banking) and to the front

Excessive braking or accelerating as you ride round a corner or bend reduces the control you have over your machine. If more tyre grip is used for braking or accelerating, there is less available for cornering and this reduces your control over the positioning of your machine. Eventually, if there is not enough tyre grip for cornering, a skid will develop. The more slippery the road surface, the earlier this will happen.

Braking is particularly hazardous on a banked machine. Moderate use of the brakes is possible on a sound surface and with experience but indicates a lack of observation and planning. Use of the brakes while cornering should be avoided. It is likely to cause the tyres to slip to the outside and the machine to drop to the inside. It is extremely destabilising because it adversely affects tyre grip, front–back load distribution and the balance of banking forces all at the same time. The only reliable way to corner safely is to adjust speed on approach to suit the surface conditions and the severity of the bend, and to maintain that speed round the bend.

The more you brake or accelerate, the less you will be able to corner safely.

Avoid braking when cornering.

As you ride round bends in the next few days, analyse what is happening to your tyre grip in terms of the trade-off between accelerating or braking on the one hand and cornering on the other. Ask yourself the following questions:

Do you finish braking before you go into a bend?

Do you avoid accelerating harshly while riding round bends?

Using the throttle

If you are in the right gear, opening the throttle will increase both engine and road speed. If you are in a gear that is too high for your speed, the engine will not be able to respond because the load from the wheels is too great. Changing to a lower gear reduces the load from the wheels, allowing the engine to speed up and so move the motorcycle faster.

When the throttle is closed the opposite effect – deceleration – occurs. The engine slows down and cylinder compression slows the motorcycle down. The lower the gear, the greater the slowing effect of the engine (because there are more compression strokes for each rotation of the wheel).

So, in the appropriate gear, the throttle has two effects:

- increase in speed when the throttle is opened
- decrease in speed when the throttle is closed.

Acceleration and machine balance

Acceleration alters the distribution of weight between the wheels of the motorcycle. When a machine accelerates the weight lifts from the front and pushes down on the back wheel, increasing the grip of the rear tyre. During deceleration the opposite happens, increasing the grip of the front tyre.

During acceleration

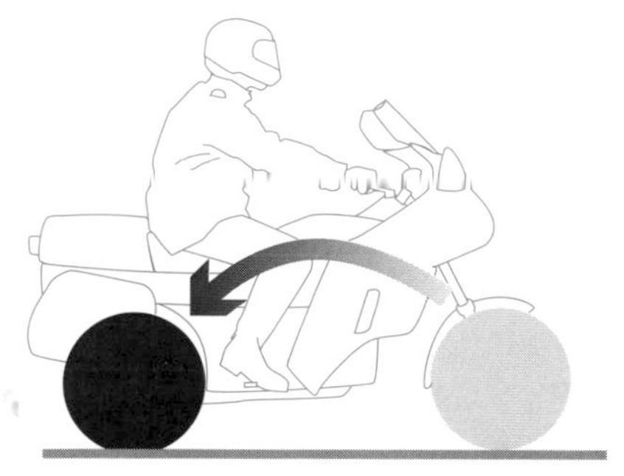

the rear tyre gains grip

the grip of the front tyre reduces

During deceleration

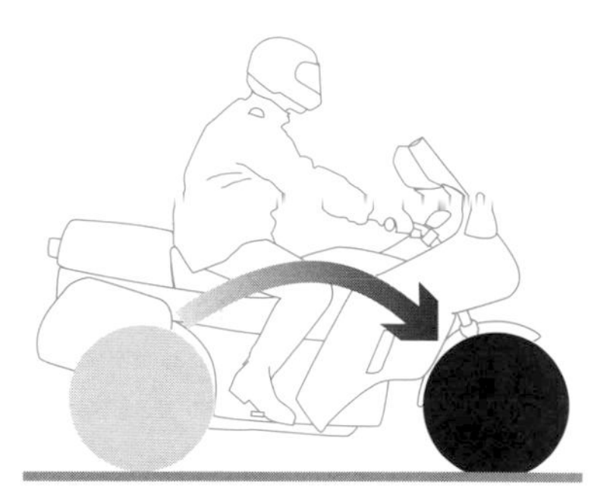

the grip of the rear tyre reduces

the front tyre gains grip

Developing your skill at using the throttle

Motorcycles are very responsive to use of the throttle during acceleration and deceleration. Depending on the grip of the road surface, excessive acceleration can lift the front wheel of the bike or cause the rear wheel to spin. Both cause loss of stability. Make sure you know the capabilities of your machine and ride within them.

Jerky use of the throttle is uncomfortable, puts unnecessary strains on the machine, and adversely affects tyre grip. It should be used deftly, using precise and smooth movements to open or close it.

Acceleration capability varies widely between machines and depends on the size of the engine, its efficiency and the power-to-weight ratio. Take time to become familiar with the acceleration capability of the machines you ride: the safety of many manoeuvres, particularly overtaking, depends on your good judgement of it.

Always consider the safety implications of accelerating. Sudden sharp movements of the throttle reduce the adhesion of the tyre to the road and jeopardise control, especially when cornering. The faster you go, the further you will travel before you can react to a hazard. You will take longer to stop and, if you do crash, your impact speed will be higher.

Acceleration sense

Acceleration sense is the ability to vary machine speed in response to changing road and traffic conditions by accurate use of the throttle. It is a key riding skill and is used in every riding situation: moving off, accelerating, slowing down, overtaking, complying with speed limits, following other traffic and negotiating hazards. It requires careful observation, good anticipation, sound judgement of speed and distance, experience and an awareness of your machine's capabilities.

A lack of acceleration sense causes many common mistakes, most importantly excessive use of the brakes. For example, when you move off from a junction, you should be able to use your throttle to catch up, and match the speed of the traffic in front, without having to use your brakes (assuming there are no sudden interruptions of the traffic flow). If you accelerate and then have to brake to adjust your speed to the vehicles in front, you are not making good use of acceleration sense. Similarly when overtaking (assuming there are no additional hazards), you should be able to move up and overtake, using your throttle to control your speed throughout. If you have to brake, to follow the vehicle in front or to get the timing right, you have miscalculated the amount of acceleration for the circumstances. Good acceleration sense helps avoid unnecessary braking, improves stability and reduces wear and tear on the machine.

As motorcycles are very responsive to the throttle, you should always be aware of the position and speed of the vehicles behind you, especially before you decelerate. Ask yourself, 'Will they have enough room to stop? Would it be wise to show the brake light to warn the vehicle behind that I am slowing down? Have I planned an escape route if they fail to slow sufficiently?'

Always comply with the basic riding safety rule: Be able to stop on your own side of the road within the distance you can see to be clear.

When you have the opportunity, ride along a regular route using acceleration sense rather than braking. Notice how it improves your anticipation and increases the smoothness of the ride.

Accelerating on bends

A moving machine is at its most stable when its weight is evenly distributed, its engine is just pulling without increasing road speed, and it is travelling in a straight line. Accelerating to increase the road speed round a bend upsets these conditions.

If you accelerate hard and alter direction at the same time you run the risk of demanding too much from the available tyre grip. If the tyres lose grip you lose cornering control. To get maximum cornering control, avoid altering your road speed at the same time as altering direction.

*See Chapter 5, **Cornering, balance and avoiding skids**, page 86, **Cornering forces**.*

As soon as a machine turns into a bend it starts to slow down due to cornering forces. If you keep a constant throttle setting into and round the bend you will lose road speed and the weight of the bike will shift to the front, affecting stability.

To get the best stability while cornering you need to keep your speed constant. Do this by opening the throttle sufficiently to compensate for the speed lost due to cornering forces. How much you open the throttle is a matter of fine judgement, but **your purpose is to maintain constant speed, not to increase it**.

When you need to corner and increase speed together, use the throttle sensitively and smoothly to keep within the tyre grip available. Use extra care in slippery conditions because misjudgement will result in wheel spin, loss of cornering control and a skid.

Follow the guiding safety principle. **Adjust your speed on the approach to bends so that you are able to stop on your own side of the road within the distance you can see to be clear**.

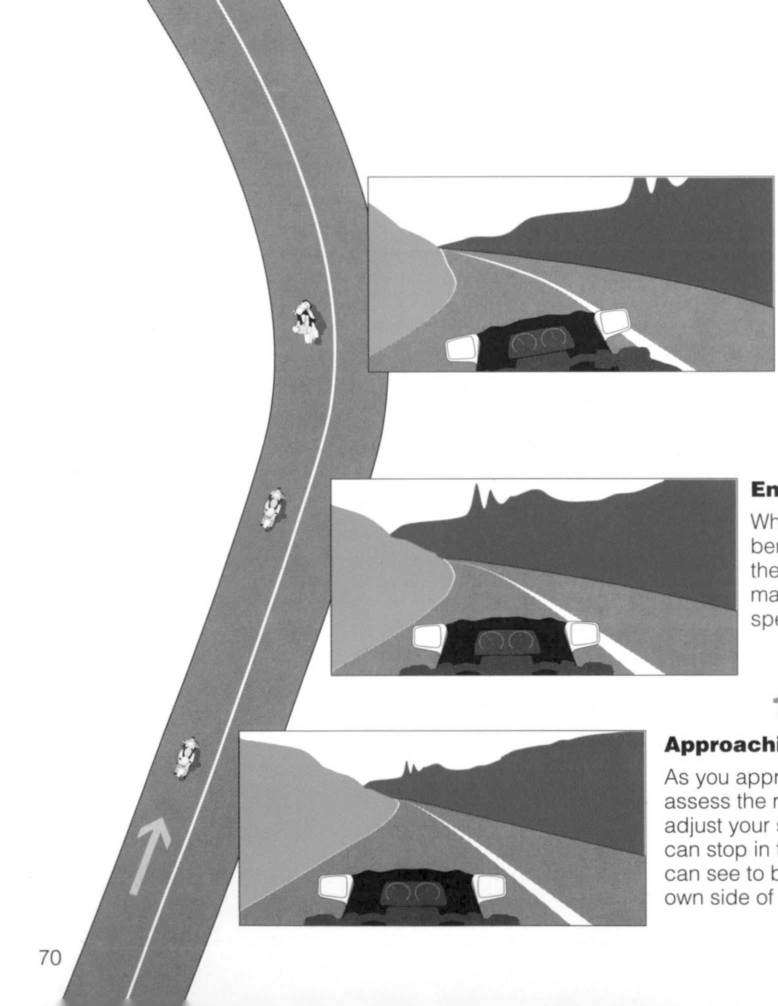

3

Coming out of the bend

As the road begins to straighten and you start to return to the upright, start to accelerate smoothly.

2

Entering the bend

While the curvature of the bend is constant, open the throttle sufficiently to maintain a constant speed round the bend.

1

Approaching the bend

As you approach the bend, assess the road surface and adjust your speed so that you can stop in the distance you can see to be clear on your own side of the road.

The key points to remember are:

- set your speed for a bend according to the overall stopping distance, taking into account the condition of the road surface and the presence of other road users
- maintain a constant speed round the bend
- the harder you accelerate, the less your cornering ability
- use the throttle smoothly – jerkiness causes wheel slip
- look carefully for signs of slippery surface conditions, and adjust your speed before you reach them.

Using the gears

The way you use your gears can make or mar your riding. Your machine can only deliver the necessary power to increase speed if you are in the right gear. Skilful use of the gears depends on choosing the right gear for the road speed, accurately matching the engine speed through the chosen gear to the road speed, and using the clutch and throttle precisely. This will deliver smooth gear changes and contribute to the stability of your ride. You should aim to:

- know the approximate maximum road speed for each gear of the machine
- make all gear changes smoothly
- be in the correct gear for the road speed and traffic situation.

Rapid progress is made by accelerating up to the engine's peak performance and changing to a higher gear. To do this you need to know the manufacturer's recommendations for the machine's peak engine performance. This may differ from both the maximum torque and the maximum revs of the engine.

You will get best use from the gears if you understand how they work. Their main purpose is to transform speed of turning into power of turning and vice versa.

- The bottom gear produces plenty of power but relatively little speed.
- The top gear produces plenty of speed but at relatively low power.

- The gears between produce varying combinations of power and speed.

To climb a steep hill the back wheel needs plenty of power. This is gained at the expense of speed by selecting a low gear. Cruising on a level stretch of motorway requires speed but relatively little power: speed is gained at the expense of power by selecting a high gear.

Rapid acceleration is achieved by selecting a lower gear. This provides more power and so can increase speed more quickly than a higher gear. The engine can only increase its speed if the load on it is not too great. A lower gear supplies more power to the wheels at a reduced load on the engine. But the top speed of a lower gear is limited and eventually you have to change to a higher gear to gain more speed: turning power is converted into speed.

The greater turning power of low gears affects tyre grip. The greater the turning power, the more likely wheel slip becomes. This is why it is advisable to use a higher gear when moving slowly in slippery conditions such as on snow, ice or mud. It is also why wheel slip occurs when you accelerate hard in first gear.

Moving off from stationary

The ideal way to move off from a standing start is to accelerate smoothly and to gather speed by steadily working up through the gears. Maximum acceleration through the gears should only be used on occasions of pressing need, and when the road surface and other conditions are right. Over-accelerating in low gears or remaining in a gear beyond the limits of its optimum performance damages the engine. For this reason some machines are fitted with rev-limiters.

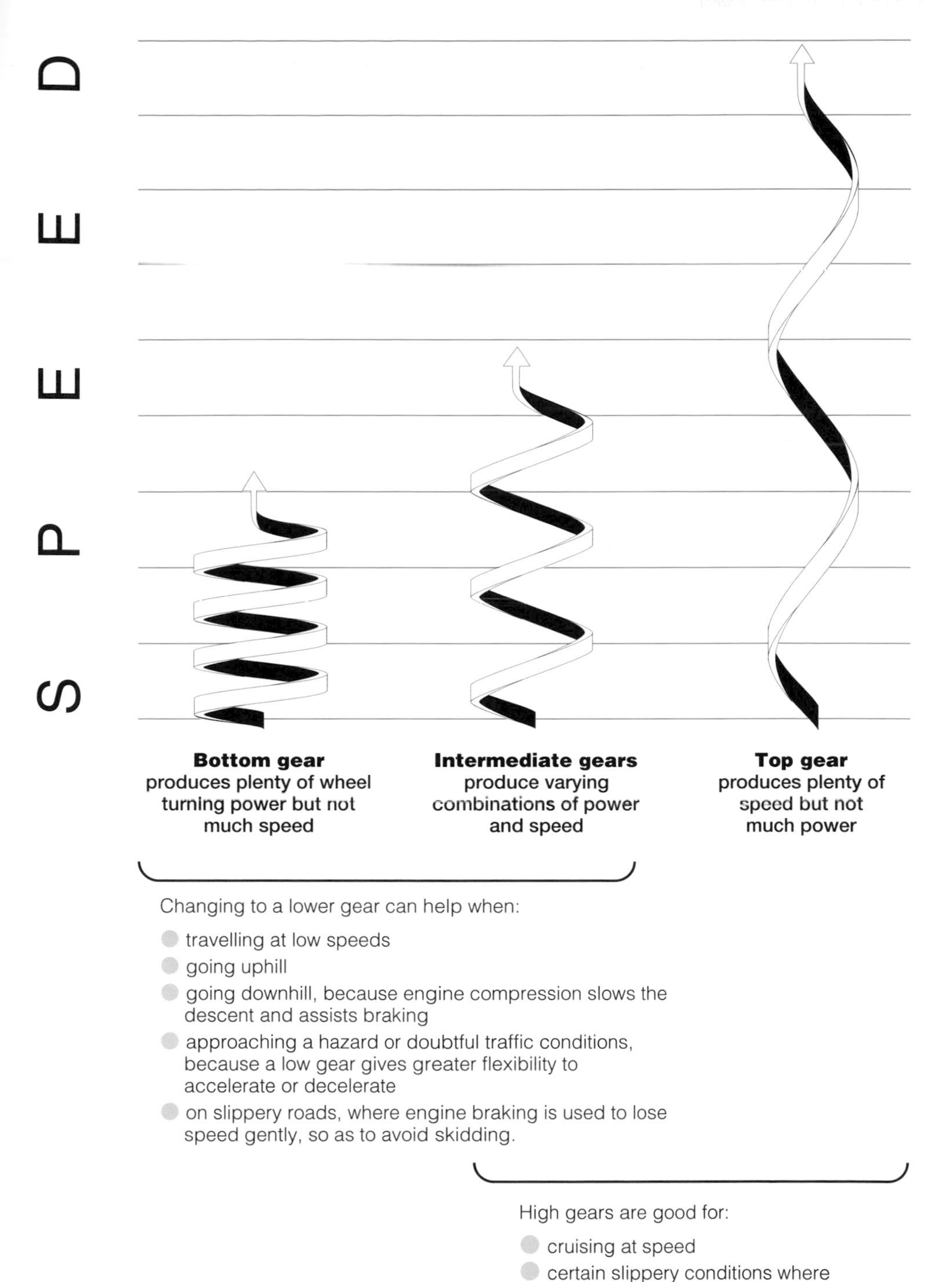

Bottom gear
produces plenty of wheel turning power but not much speed

Intermediate gears
produce varying combinations of power and speed

Top gear
produces plenty of speed but not much power

Changing to a lower gear can help when:

- travelling at low speeds
- going uphill
- going downhill, because engine compression slows the descent and assists braking
- approaching a hazard or doubtful traffic conditions, because a low gear gives greater flexibility to accelerate or decelerate
- on slippery roads, where engine braking is used to lose speed gently, so as to avoid skidding.

High gears are good for:

- cruising at speed
- certain slippery conditions where lower gears may cause wheel spin.

Braking and changing gear

The sequential gearbox on a bike does not allow intermediate gears to be missed when changing up or down. When speed is lost through braking, multiple changing down of gears is often required. There are two techniques which can be used to do this:

- block changing
- sequential changing.

If, because of inadequate planning, you brake late and rush a gear change, you risk destabilising your machine exactly when you need the greatest stability for negotiating the hazard.

Block changing

During the later stages of braking, hold in the clutch lever and change down the gears until the appropriate lower gear is selected, then release the clutch.

This technique allows rapid movement through the gears, but depends on correctly choosing the appropriate gear for the road speed and accurately counting the gears. If too low a gear is selected there is a risk of locking the rear wheel and causing a skid.

Sequential changing

As speed is lost during braking, work down through each gear, engaging the next lower gear as its optimum speed range is entered.

At each stage, accurately match the engine speed and gear to the road speed. This promotes smoothness and avoids locking the rear wheel.

With this technique, engine braking helps to slow the machine. The appropriate gear for the speed is engaged throughout, and because the drive is engaged except during changes, the bike remains stable. The rider also has the option of immediate power if needed.

Riders should be able to use both techniques but whichever you use, it must be properly incorporated into your planning.

Key pointers to skilful gear use

- Recognise when to change gear by the sound of the engine.
- Choose the right gear for the road speed.
- Develop good coordination of hand and foot movements.
- Brake in good time to slow to the right road speed as you approach a hazard, and passing through the intermediate gears, select the appropriate gear.
- Use the brakes rather than the gears to slow the machine (except during hill descents and when there is a risk of skidding).

How well do you use your gears?

Ask yourself the following questions as you ride.

Are you always in the right gear?

Do you avoid using your gears to slow down except on hills and slippery surfaces?

Do you ever find yourself changing gear halfway round a corner?

Generally, avoid changing gear while cornering because it destabilises the machine.

Slowing down and stopping

You need to be able to slow down or stop your machine with it fully under control. The smoothness of a ride is greatly improved by early anticipation of the need to slow down or stop, and by slowing gently and progressively. The ability to accurately estimate the required stopping distance at different speeds and in different conditions is a central skill of safe riding, and one which you should strive to develop. There are three ways of slowing down or stopping:

- decelerating (closing the throttle)
- using the gears (recommended only in slippery conditions)
- using the brakes.

Deceleration

Deceleration (often called engine braking) is an important way of slowing a bike. When you close the throttle the engine slows and by means of engine compression it slows the rear wheel. This reduces road speed smoothly and gradually with little wear to the machine. The lower the gear the greater the loss of road speed.

If the throttle is closed smoothly, engine braking provides a steady and smooth braking effect. It is particularly useful in conditions where the brakes might lock the wheels – on slippery roads, for example. Engine braking is also used on long descents in hilly country.

Engine braking operates only on the rear wheel. Despite this, it is a very effective way of losing speed. You should consider rear observation whenever you plan to use it.

Using the gears

The use of the gears to slow down in slippery conditions requires sensitive control of the throttle and clutch. The technique makes use of the greater engine braking capability of lower gears. It operates only on the rear wheel.

To use this technique, select a lower gear and, before the clutch is released, use the throttle to match the engine speed to the selected gear and road speed. Release the clutch smoothly. After the clutch is fully released, reduce road speed by gradually closing the throttle. Any jerkiness caused by mismatching the engine speed to the road speed, using the clutch unevenly or decelerating too rapidly, risks causing a skid.

See Chapter 5, ***Cornering, balance and avoiding skids****.*

Using the brakes

Use the brakes when you need to slow more quickly than you are able to using engine braking. Correct use of the brakes on a bike can slow you quickly and effectively. Incorrect use can cause you to collide or lose control of your machine unnecessarily. Research shows that 19% of all riders do not use their front brakes even in an emergency. Other research estimated that 30% of accidents could have been avoided if the brakes had been used to their full capacity.

Follow these guidelines for braking:

- brake firmly only when travelling in a straight line
- brake in plenty of time
- adjust brake pressure to the condition of the road surface
- avoid using the front brake
  – when the machine is banked
  – when turning
  – on loose or slippery surfaces
- on hills, brake on the straight stretches and ease off on the bends.

Brakes on a bike

The front wheel produces a larger braking effort than the rear wheel.

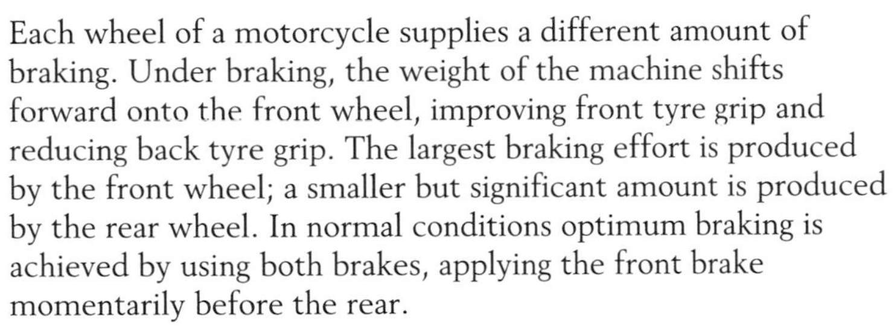

Each wheel of a motorcycle supplies a different amount of braking. Under braking, the weight of the machine shifts forward onto the front wheel, improving front tyre grip and reducing back tyre grip. The largest braking effort is produced by the front wheel; a smaller but significant amount is produced by the rear wheel. In normal conditions optimum braking is achieved by using both brakes, applying the front brake momentarily before the rear.

Braking effort has to be applied to the two wheels with great sensitivity and discrimination. The shift in weight off the rear tyre onto the front tyre means that it is relatively easy to exceed the amount of tyre grip available at the rear tyre. Excessive pressure on the rear brake will cause the rear tyre to lock. On a bend this will cause the back end to swing out and will destabilise the sideways balance of the machine.

Some riders are reluctant to use the front brake in any conditions because they fear the possibility of locking the front wheel. This means they lose most of their braking capability. There are a number of situations where you are advised to avoid using the front brake but this is not rigid advice. As you develop experience and your feel for your machine improves, you will develop the ability to use the front brake in adverse situations. It is a question of your awareness of the tolerances of tyre grip and of your finesse in operating the controls. Reliance on the rear brake alone has serious disadvantages. Using it alone, especially under hard braking, causes the rear wheel to rise, lock and bounce along the road. This greatly extends the braking distance and destabilises the bike.

The best combination of front and rear braking varies with speed, direction of travel, and road surface conditions. General advice on which combination to use is given below:

When to apply the brakes and by how much depends on your speed, the space available, the road surface and your assessment of the appropriate speed for approaching the hazard. Braking should normally be progressive and increased steadily until most of the unwanted speed has been lost; pressure on the brakes should then be decreased to ensure maximum smoothness.

Gently take up the initial free movement of the brakes

Distribute and increase pressures progressively as required

Relax pressures as unwanted road speed is lost

Release the pressure just before stopping to avoid a jerking halt

---

Do you know the braking capabilities of the machines you ride?

Find a suitable location,with clear views and where you can test your brakes without affecting other road users.

Practise using your brakes:

- **use both brakes together**
- **use the front brake on its own**
- **use the rear brake on its own.**

If you have ABS or coupled brakes follow the manufacturer's guidance on braking.

These trials should give you the confidence to use your brakes to the full when necessary. However always be aware of the effects of cornering and slippery surfaces on your ability to brake without locking the wheels.

During cornering

Braking is hazardous during cornering because it affects the stability of the machine and may cause the wheels to slide sideways. If this happens there is always the possibility that the machine may fall over. If braking is necessary, brake gently and steadily. Adjust the brake pressure according to the condition of the road surface and avoid locking the wheels.

See **The tyre grip trade-off** above, page 65.

Generally, plan to brake in plenty of time on the approach to a corner or bend. Avoid braking while cornering.

On poor surfaces

Where the surface of the road is poor and grip is reduced, for example, because of loose gravel, damp, rain, road paint, leaves or dust, brake on the part of the road that provides the best grip. Adjust the intensity of your braking according to the immediate surface conditions, increasing pressure on a good surface, reducing pressure on a poor one. Where the surface is uncertain, avoid using the brakes and rely on engine braking to slow down. Gently use the back brake to bring the bike to a final halt.

See Chapter 3, **Observation**.

This level of response to surface conditions requires intense observation and intelligent anticipation.

Emergency braking on a good dry road

In an emergency, assess whether you can steer out of trouble or whether you have room to brake to a standstill on a straight course. The quickest and shortest way to stop on a good dry road is to brake to a point just before the wheels lock (technically, the point at which there is 15% wheel slip). Brake as firmly as possible with both brakes but avoid locking either wheel. As the machine slows gradually relax the pressure on the front brake and increase the pressure on the rear brake.

If the machine is banked, and time and space permit, try to return the bike upright. Apply the rear brake and avoid using the front brake until the bike is upright. If there is a choice between braking hard or colliding, apply the rear brake hard and lean the machine further over. If the front brake is used other than lightly, tyre grip will be lost and the machine will slide outwards.

On machines fitted with an antilock braking system, firmly apply the brakes. Do not release them as you feel the system come into operation. The brakes need to be fully applied for the system to work. Do not be alarmed by the pulsing sensation felt while ABS is operating.

Emergency braking on a slippery road

Emergency braking on a slippery surface should be avoided wherever possible. It is much better to avoid having to brake in these conditions by using thorough observation, anticipation, and early adjustment of speed. If it is necessary to brake and the machine is upright, distribute your braking effort almost equally between the front and rear brakes. When the machine is banked, only use the front brake as a last resort.

Machines fitted with linked brakes and an antilock braking system can be braked heavily when upright on a slippery surface and remain stable. However, braking distances are greatly increased. This technology does not justify poor riding technique or taking greater risks.

*See Chapter 5, **Cornering, balance and avoiding skids**.*

Testing your brakes

Every time you use your machine check that the brakes work. Do a stationary check before you move off, and check them again when you are moving.

- **The stationary test**. Check that the hand lever and foot pedal move freely and give a firm positive pressure.
- **The moving test**. Make sure that the brakes are working efficiently under running conditions. Choose a flat, level road with good surface conditions and no other traffic. Bring the speed up and apply both brakes. Adjust your braking effort to the existing surface conditions. Until you have done this test keep your speeds low and brake early for any hazards.

  If you are on the same machine all day you only need to do this test once, provided you have no reason to suspect the performance of the brakes. Always consider the safety and convenience of other road users before you do a moving test.

The safe stopping distance rule

This is one of the guiding principles of *Motorcycle Roadcraft* and should always be observed. By relating your speed to the distance in which you can stop, you can assess the safety of your speed in any situation.

Never ride so fast that you cannot stop comfortably on your own side of the road within the distance you can see to be clear.

The importance of this rule for your own and other people's safety cannot be overstated. It provides a guide to the speed at which you should corner, and it indicates the speed and distance you should keep from other vehicles in all other traffic situations. Successfully applying this rule requires skill. You need to be aware of:

- the braking capabilities of your machine
- the type and condition of the road surface – in slippery or wet conditions braking distances increase greatly
- the effects of cornering, braking and machine balance on tyre grip.

The only variation to this rule occurs in narrow and single track lanes where you need to allow twice the overall stopping distance that you can see to be clear. This is to allow sufficient room for any oncoming vehicle to see you and also brake.

Overall safe stopping distance

To work out the overall safe stopping distance add thinking distance to braking distance.

Thinking distance + Braking distance = Stopping distance

- **Thinking distance** is the distance travelled in the time between first observing the need for action and acting. The average rider reacts to expected events in 0.7 seconds. The distance covered in that time is the same figure in feet (0.3m) as the speed in miles per hour; for example, at 30 miles per hour thinking distance is 30 feet (9m).

  Actual thinking distance varies according to the speed of the machine, your physical and mental condition, your attentiveness and whether or not you are expecting something to happen. Everyone takes much longer to react to unexpected events than to expected ones.

- **Braking distance** is the distance needed for braking in dry conditions. You should be familiar with the braking distances for different speeds recommended in the *Highway Code*.

  Actual braking distance depends on the machine's capability, the gradient of the road, the condition of the road surface and how you use the brakes. Rising or falling gradients have a significant effect on deceleration and braking distances. Slippery surfaces greatly increase braking distances.

The two-second rule

One way of keeping a safe distance on fast roads is by leaving a gap of at least two seconds between you and the vehicle in front. An easy way to count two seconds is to say:

Only a fool breaks the two-second rule.

This time should be at least doubled in wet weather and further increased in icy conditions. If the vehicle behind you is too close, drop back further from the vehicle in front. This will allow you to brake more gently in an emergency and may prevent you being rammed from behind.

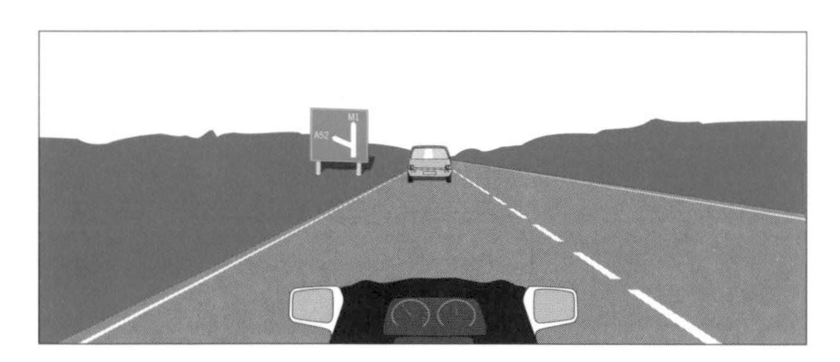

Note when the car in front passes a convenient landmark.

Count one second

Count two seconds

If you pass the object before you have counted two seconds, you are too close. Drop back and try the test again.

Do you know your safe stopping distance?

23m, 53m and 96m are the respective shortest stopping distances at 30, 50, and 70 mph.

Do you know what these stopping distances actually look like on the ground? Work out your own pace length (usually less than 1m) and then pace out the three distances. Do this somewhere familiar so that you have a permanent mental image of them.

Do you generally avoid braking when going round corners?

See Chapter 2, *The system of motorcycle control*.

Braking as you approach a hazard

To apply the system of motorcycle control you should consider your road speed on the approach to a hazard and adjust it if necessary. If you need to slow down, consider rear observation, adopt the best road position and then reduce speed safely and smoothly using deceleration, braking or a combination of both.

When and how firmly you apply the brakes depends on your judgement of speed and distance. You should consider:

- your initial speed
- the road surface
- the degree of cornering
- weather conditions
- the specific road and traffic conditions

Sometimes braking may need to be firm but it should never be harsh. Harsh braking usually indicates poor observation, anticipation and planning. Aim to lose speed *steadily* from the first moment until you achieve the right speed to negotiate the hazard. Timing is crucial: avoid braking so early that you have to re-accelerate to reach the hazard, or so late that you have to brake forcefully.

Review

In this chapter we have looked at:

- improving your skill in using the basic controls for moving and stopping a machine
- how to get the maximum safety out of the tyre grip available on your machine
- how acceleration and braking affect machine balance
- how to use the gears in different circumstances
- the importance of engine braking on a bike
- how to use the brakes on a bike
- testing your brakes
- why stopping distance is so important, and how to assess safe braking distances.

Check your understanding

How and why does acceleration affect your ability to corner?

How and why does braking affect your ability to corner?

Why do you need to be in the right gear to accelerate?

What is the basic riding safety rule?

When, if at all, should you use your gears to brake?

What is the safest way to lose speed gently in slippery conditions?

How do you calculate overall stopping distance?

What are the factors that affect thinking distance and braking distance?

What are the key points to remember concerning the distribution of braking effort between the front and the back wheels?

If you have difficulty in answering any of these questions, look back over the relevant part of this chapter to refresh your memory.

Use this chapter to find out:

- the principles of cornering
- the forces involved in cornering
- the factors which affect your bike's ability to corner
- the role of balance in cornering
- how to use the limit point to judge your speed for a corner
- how to use the system of motorcycle control for cornering
- the best course to take round a bend
- how to avoid skidding
- what causes a skid
- how to correct a skid.

Chapter 5

Cornering, balance and avoiding skids

The first part of this chapter explains how to apply the system of motorcycle control to cornering. The second part explains how to avoid and deal with skids.

Developing your skill at cornering and balance

'Cornering' means riding a motorcycle round a corner, curve or bend. Cornering is one of the main riding activities, and it is important to get it right. When you corner, your machine loses stability, and you place extra demands on the tyre grip available. The faster you go and the tighter the bend, the greater these demands are.

*See Chapter 2, **The system of motorcycle control**.*

Every bend is different and varies with the traffic and weather, but the first section sets out the general principles of cornering that will help you to ride round all corners and bends safely.

The following sections explain the forces involved in cornering; the factors that can increase or reduce your bike's ability to corner safely; and how to use the system of motorcycle control in conjunction with limit point analysis. This technique, used together with good observation and the system of motorcycle control, provides a clear and consistent way of assessing safe cornering speeds.

The system of motorcycle control – principles for safe cornering

Cornering is potentially dangerous so you should use the system of motorcycle control to help you carry out the manoeuvre safely. Each phase of the system is relevant, but the information phase is especially important. Correctly assessing the severity of the bend is essential for safety. Applying the system and the safe stopping rule gives us four key principles of safe cornering:

- your machine should be in the right position on the approach
- you should be travelling at the right speed for the corner or bend
- you should have the right gear for that speed
- you should be able to stop on your own side of the road in the distance you can see to be clear.

Applying these principles to the variations in bend, traffic conditions, road surface conditions, visibility and other factors requires good judgement and planning. But before we look in more detail at using the system of motorcycle control for cornering, it is helpful to consider the other key factors that affect a bike's ability to corner safely.

Think back to any occasions when you have experienced a loss of control while cornering. For each occasion work out why this happened and how you could prevent it happening again.

Examine each situation for the influence of the following factors:

- poor general observation
- poor observation of the road surface
- poor anticipation
- poor planning.

Cornering forces

A moving motorcycle is at its most stable when travelling in a straight line on a level course and at constant speed. It will continue to travel on a straight course unless some other force is applied to alter its direction. When you steer, the turning force to alter direction comes from the action of the front tyre on the road. We saw in Chapter 4 that this force depends on tyre grip. If the front tyre grip is broken, the motorcycle will continue in a straight line. On tighter bends, at higher speeds and with heavier machines, the demands on tyre grip are greater.

When you corner you need to balance the machine by leaning to the inside of the curve. If you did not do this the machine would fall to the outside of the curve. Leaning makes use of gravity to maintain stability.

You will recall from Chapter 4 that tyre grip faces competing demands from three actions:

- cornering
- accelerating
- braking.

The more you brake or accelerate, the less tyre grip you have for cornering. The faster you go into a corner or bend, the greater the tyre grip required to keep you on course round it.

The practical outcome of these forces is to cause a machine to continue in a straight line and possibly fall over whenever tyre grip is lost. So in a left-hand bend, as tyre grip is lost, your bike drifts to the right of your intended course, and in a right-hand bend it drifts to the left. The design of the machine and tyres will reduce or accentuate these tendencies.

Tendency of a motorcycle to continue in a straight line

Machine characteristics

Roadworthiness

Machines vary in their ability to corner, and they only corner to the best of their ability if they are well maintained. Steering, suspension, tyres, tyre pressures and the loading of the machine all affect its balance and road grip when cornering. Make sure that your bike and tyres are in good condition, and that your tyre pressures are kept at the recommended levels – condition and pressures are very important for motorcycle tyres. Also position any loads so that they do not upset the balance of the bike or restrict any moving parts.

Machine specification

The specifications that affect the road holding and handling characteristics of a machine vary considerably. You should make it a priority to be familiar with the characteristics of any machine you ride. They include:

- the make and type of tyres
- the suspension and damping settings
- traction control, if fitted
- the type of final drive (chain or shaft).

Cornering and balance

The front wheel of a motorcycle is only turned significantly to change direction at very low speeds. The machine and rider remain virtually upright and the demands on tyre grip are minimal. The rider unconsciously maintains balance by making small adjustments to body position and pressure on handlebars.

See Cornering forces, page 86.

At higher speeds the rider needs to lean into the bend to counterbalance the perceived effect of body and bike flying outwards.

The sharper the bend or the higher the speed, the greater the required degree of lean to maintain balance. As cornering effort and banking is increased, a point will be reached where tyre grip is lost or the machine touches the road surface – potentially causing loss of control.

As the machine comes out of the bend, the rider must steadily

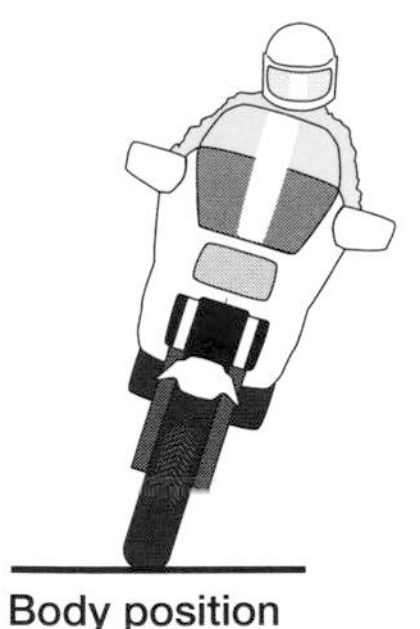
Body position during banking

return to an upright position to maintain balance. If the rider continued to lean at the same angle while cornering forces were reduced, the machine would fall over in the direction of the lean.

Riding position and balance

The way you sit on a bike affects its balance and handling.

When the bike is stationary you should be able either to place both feet on the ground or balance with one foot while the other works a control.

After moving off, place both feet on the foot pegs, with the insteps resting on the pegs. Do this as soon as possible because it improves stability and control and reduces fatigue. When you are moving, sit in a comfortable position with your body slightly leaning forward. Sit so that you can reach the controls comfortably without locking your arms straight. A slight bend to your arms will prevent the transmission of shock from the handlebars to the rest of your body and the bike.

Camber and superelevation

The road surface is not normally level across its width but is built with a slope to assist drainage. The slope across the road affects steering. The normal slope falls from the crown of the road to the edges and is called camber.

On a left-hand bend camber assists cornering because the road slopes down in the direction of turn, and reduces the angle between the tyre and the road surface – increasing the area of contact between them.

On a right-hand bend camber reduces the stability of cornering because the road slopes away from the direction of turn, and increases the angle between the tyre and the road surface – reducing the area of contact between them.

This advice applies to normal camber only if you keep to your own side of the road.

There are many instances, especially at junctions, where the slope across the road surface is at an unexpected angle. Whatever the slope, if it falls in the direction of your turn it will increase the effect of your steering; if it rises in the direction of your turn it will reduce the effect of your steering. You need to consider the slope across the road when deciding on your speed for a bend.

Superelevation is where the whole width of the road is banked up towards the outside edge of the bend, making the slope favourable for cornering in both directions.

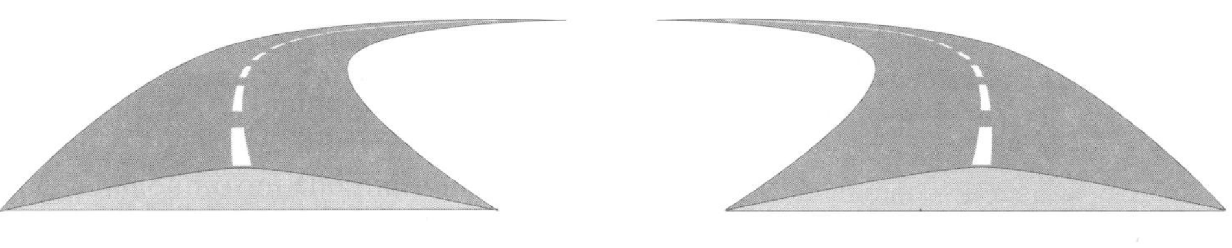

Crown camber

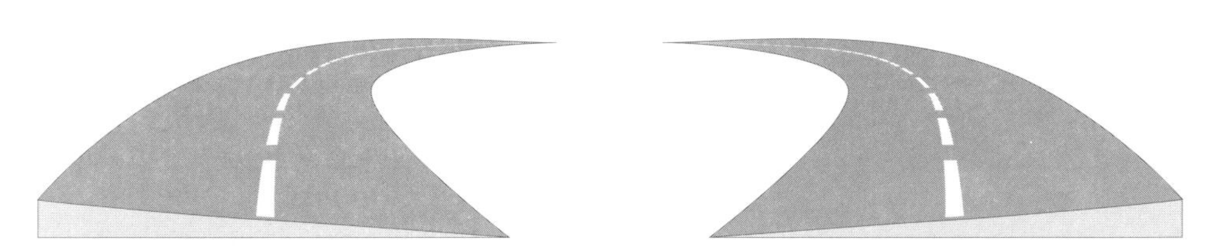

Superelevation

Next time you make a short journey, observe the camber every time you corner.

Can you identify three sections of road on any of the routes that you regularly use where the slope across the road surface makes cornering difficult?

As you go round bends observe the effect of the camber on your cornering and notice its effect on the steering and balance of your machine.

Summary of factors affecting cornering

To sum up, the factors that determine your machine's ability to corner are:

- speed
- the amount of lean you apply
- the amount of acceleration or braking
- the slope across the road surface – camber and superelevation
- the road surface and how the weather and other factors have affected its grip
- the characteristics of the machine and its ground clearance
- the weight and distribution of any load carried
- the rider's ability.

The system of motorcycle control and the limit point

Now that you can identify the factors which affect your machine's ability to corner, the following section explains in detail how to use the system of motorcycle control and the limit point to corner safely.

The system of motorcycle control assists planning in approaching and negotiating corners and bends. The five phases of the system – information, position, speed, gear and acceleration – highlight the essential factors that you must consider when cornering.

As you approach a bend using the system you should be seeking as much information as possible about the severity of the bend and the state of the road surface. You should use all the observational aids and clues available to you (weather, road signs, road markings, the line made by lamp posts and trees, the speed and position of oncoming traffic, the angle of headlights at night, etc) to anticipate and plan for the severity of the bend. A valuable aid to observation is the limit point because it gives you a systematic way of judging the correct speed through the bend.

How to use the limit point to help you corner

The limit point is the furthest point along a road to which you have an uninterrupted view of the road surface. On a level stretch of road this will be where the right-hand side of the road appears to intersect with the left-hand side of the road. This point of intersection is known as the limit point. To ride safely you must be able to stop on your own side of the road within the distance you can see to be clear – that is, the distance between you and the limit point.

The ability to stop on your own side of the road in the distance you can see to be clear determines how fast you can go. The more distant the limit point, the faster you can go because you have more space to stop in. The closer the limit point, the slower you must go because you have less space to stop in.

Match your speed to the speed at which the limit point moves away from you, providing you can stop within the distance that you can see to be clear.

As you approach and go through a bend the limit point appears at first to remain stationary, then to move away at a constant speed and finally to sprint away to the horizon as you come out of the bend. The technique of limit point analysis is to match your speed to the speed at which the limit point appears to move. If it is moving away from you, accelerate. If it is coming closer to you or standing still, decelerate or brake. Even if the bend is not constant, you can still match your speed to the apparent movement of the limit point, because this will vary with the curvature of the bend.

Approaching the bend

- At first the limit point appears to remain at the same point in the road. Reduce your speed to be able to stop safely within the remaining distance.
- As you approach the bend take information about the sharpness of the bend and carefully assess the appropriate speed for cornering.

1

2

3

Going through the bend

- Just before you enter the bend the limit point begins to move round at a constant speed. Adjust your speed and gear, if necessary, to the speed of this movement.
- You now have the correct speed and gear for the bend. Select the gear to match the speed *before* entering the bend.

4

5

6

Coming out of the bend

- As the bend starts to straighten, your view begins to extend and the limit point starts to move away more quickly. As your machine straightens and returns to an upright position, increase your acceleration towards the limit point.
- As the bend comes to an end, continue to accelerate to catch the limit point until other considerations such as speed limits or new hazards restrict your acceleration.

7

8

9

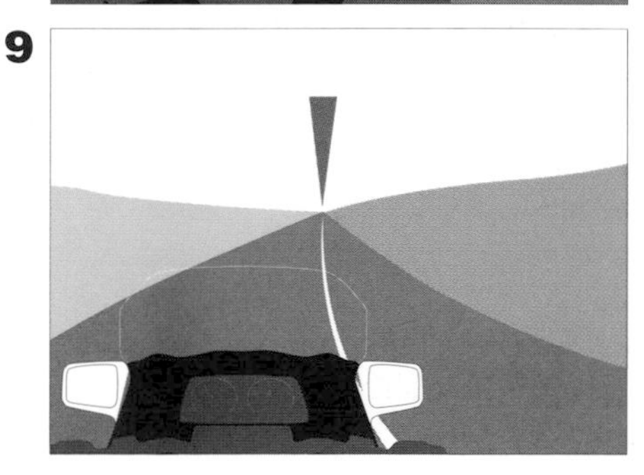

These are the advantages of using the limit point together with the system:

- it ensures that you observe the riding safety rule of matching your speed to your ability to stop within the distance you can see to be clear
- it gives you the appropriate speed to approach and negotiate the bend
- it gives you the appropriate speed to go round the bend, and therefore the appropriate gear to be in
- it gives the point at which to start to accelerating
- it is self-adjusting: as road surface conditions deteriorate, more distance is needed in which to stop; as visibility reduces so does the distance that can be seen to be clear. In both cases you need to reduce your speed to compensate.

Over the next two weeks practise matching your road speed to the movement of the limit point. Remember to adjust your speed so that you are able to stop on your own side of the road in the distance you can see to be clear.

Make a special point of using the limit point to set your speed for bends and corners on roads you know well. It is on familiar routes that attention often wanders.

How to use the system for cornering

This section takes you through the five phases of the system, identifying key considerations at each phase and explaining how to use limit point analysis in the speed phase. As with any other use of the system, you should work through it methodically, selecting the phases that are appropriate.

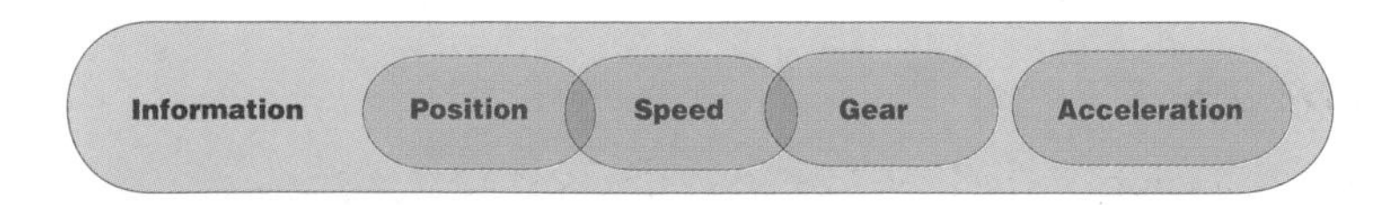

Information phase

On the approach to a corner or bend you should be constantly scanning the road for information, but specifically you need to look for:

- the traffic in front and behind
- the road surface and the effect of weather conditions on it
- the severity of the bend
- the limit point.

Seek out opportunities to look across the bend through gaps in hedges or between buildings. Look at the line of curvature of hedgerows and lamp posts to give you more information about the severity of the bend. But avoid becoming preoccupied with the bend – look for early warning of other hazards as well. If you intend to significantly alter your position to get a better view remember to take rear observation first.

Position phase

There is great flexibility in positioning a motorcycle; you should use this to compensate for your increased vulnerability as a rider. You need to consider four things when deciding where to position your machine for cornering:

- safety
- stability
- information needs
- reducing the tightness of the bend.

Safety

Position yourself so that you are least likely to come into conflict with other road users: for example, look out for pedestrians to your nearside and oncoming traffic to your offside. **Safety is the overriding consideration**. If you can safely adopt one of the positions suggested on the next page, do so, but never sacrifice safety for position.

See Chapter 3, ***Observation****, page 53,* ***Road surface*** *and* ***Reducing the tightness of the bend,*** *page 97.*

Stability

Select a course which will provide the best tyre grip.

Information needs

Your road position will determine how much you can see when you enter a bend. The position which gives you the greatest view depends on whether the bend is a left-hand bend or a right-hand bend.

- **Right-hand bends** – position yourself towards the left of your road space. Be wary of parked vehicles and pedestrians and give them sufficient clearance. Other hazards to consider before you adopt this position are:

  – blind junctions or exits

  – adverse cambers

  – poor surface conditions towards the edge of the road.

For right-hand bends, the nearside gives an earlier view into the bend.

- **Left-hand bends** – position yourself towards the centre line so that you get an early view round the bend. Before you adopt this position consider:

  – approaching traffic and other offside dangers which require a greater margin of safety

  – whether your position might mislead other traffic as to your intentions

  – whether any advantage would be gained at low speed or on an open bend (one with unrestricted views across the bend).

For left-hand bends, a position towards the centre of the road gives an earlier view.

Reducing the tightness of the bend

The other thing to consider is reducing the tightness of the curve through which you ride. By moving your bike from one side of your road space to the other you can follow a shallower curve and thereby improve stability. The path you take is different for a right- or a left-hand bend, but always consider safety first. Do not take a straighter course unless you can see clearly across the bend. Often you will not be able to do this until the road begins to straighten out.

Riding through a series of bends

Try to plan your course through a series of bends so that the exit point from the first bend puts you in a good position to enter the second bend. Only link the bends in this way if you can see clearly across them and know that there are no additional hazards. Be careful of approaching the centre line if there is the possibility of oncoming traffic. In planning your course through a series of bends ask yourself, 'Where do I want to be to approach the next bend?' Remember never to sacrifice safety for position.

When you are cornering, practise using your available road space to improve your ability to observe, and to reduce the curvature of the bend. Make sure there is no possibility of coming into conflict with other road users and that your chosen course has a sound surface.

Do this consistently for three days. Notice how it improves your ability to see, and the smoothness and stability of the ride.

Speed phase

When you have adopted an appropriate position, the next phase of the system is to consider and obtain the appropriate speed to enter the bend.

Use the limit point to judge the safe speed to ride round the bend. Where the curve round the bend is constant, the limit point moves away from you at a constant speed. This gives you the speed for the bend unless the curvature changes. If the bend tightens, the limit point appears to move closer to you, and you should reduce your speed accordingly to remain within the safe stopping distance.

When assessing the speed to go round a bend, you need to consider:

- your own ability
- your bike's characteristics
- your view into and round the bend
- the road and road surface conditions
- the traffic conditions
- the weather conditions.

When you assess the situation, do not think, 'What is the fastest that I can go round this bend?' but rather, 'Can I stop in the distance I can see to be clear?' – that is, just before the limit point.

Gear phase

During the final stage of speed adjustment before entering the bend, select the appropriate gear for that speed. Select the gear that gives you greatest flexibility.

Think also about your expected acceleration on the far side of the bend. If you expect to come out of the bend into a 30 mph area, then acceleration is often unnecessary. If the speed restriction on the other side of the bend is the national speed limit, consider entering the bend in a gear that will provide suitable acceleration to the speed limit. The condition of the road surface needs to be included in these considerations: in wet or slippery conditions, harsh acceleration in a low gear may well result in wheel spin and a loss of stability and directional control.

See Chapter 4 ***Acceleration, using gears and braking,*** *page 71,* ***Using the gears***.

Acceleration phase

Open the throttle sufficiently to maintain a constant speed round the bend. This will contribute to stability.

Providing there are no additional hazards, start to accelerate when the limit point begins to move away and you begin to bring the machine upright.

As you continue to straighten your machine, increase your acceleration to 'catch' the limit point. Accelerate until you reach the speed limit or other considerations restrict your speed.

Avoiding skids

Riding safely within the limits of the road conditions so that you are able to avoid a skid is much better than having to correct one. However skilful you are, skidding is extremely hazardous and the chances of regaining control are limited. But if you are faced with a developing skid you need to know exactly what to do to try to regain control, and how to avoid making the skid worse.

Because skidding should never be practised on a public road there are no suggestions for practising techniques in this section.

This section explains the principles and techniques for correcting a skid, but bear in mind that each skid is unique and each machine responds differently to skids. How you apply the principles and techniques will depend entirely on the circumstances and on the machine you are riding. The best way to gain confidence in dealing with a skid is through formal loose surface riding instruction.

Developments in machine design

Manufacturers are constantly seeking to improve machine safety. Antilock braking systems, linked braking and traction control systems are safety devices that can help stability. Machines fitted with these features behave differently from other machines and require different techniques to get the best use from them.

Antilock braking systems (ABS)

An increasing number of machines are fitted with an automatic antilock braking system. The purpose of ABS is to retain tyre grip during harsh or emergency braking.

ABS helps the rider to brake strongly without wheel lock when travelling in a straight line. In principle the wheels should never lock, but on a slippery surface the wheels may not rotate immediately the braking pressure is released, allowing momentary lock-up. Also during cornering the cornering forces can disrupt the system, allowing wheel lock to occur. Once ABS is activated, the rider should maintain maximum pressure on the relevant brake or brakes throughout the braking.

ABS does no more than provide the rider with an additional safety device. It does not increase the grip of the tyres on the road, nor can it prevent skidding. In limited circumstances a machine equipped with ABS can stop within a shorter distance than if the wheels were locked, but it does not reduce, and could increase, the stopping distance on a slippery surface.

For many riders ABS is a real benefit, especially when combined with a linked (front-to-back) braking system. This is because most riders are reluctant to use the full braking potential of their machines for fear of locking their wheels. ABS reduces this worry, encouraging fuller use of the brakes. It is important to get the right attitude to ABS: it does not allow you to ride faster in slippery conditions nor to be less observant. Activation of the system suggests that you are not riding safely.

Linked, coupled or combined braking systems

The front and rear brakes on most machines operate independently. Even experienced riders sometimes have difficulty achieving the optimum balance of braking effort between the two wheels. A linked or combined system links the brakes so that operation of one brake control activates both brakes in a predetermined optimum combination. On some machines both brake controls are linked to both brakes, on others only one brake control is linked to both brakes. The combination of linked brakes (front-to-rear) and ABS has been shown to provide a significant braking improvement on slippery surfaces for the average rider.

Traction control systems

Traction control systems control excess wheel slip on the rear wheel under engine acceleration, thereby improving directional control and machine stability. The systems monitor wheel slip (wheel spin) on the rear wheel and reduce the power supply to the wheel when slip exceeds a preset maximum. This allows the wheels to regain traction (or grip) and stability. It allows the machine to make maximum use of tyre grip, especially on slippery surfaces.

Controlling wheel slip is fundamentally different in a machine fitted with traction control. Different manufacturers use different systems, so **if your machine has traction control you must consult your machine handbook and follow the manufacturer's advice on what to do in skid situations**.

What causes a skid?

See Chapter 4, *Acceleration, using gears and braking*, page 76, *Using the brakes*.

Many people when asked what causes a skid would say that it was the result of poor road or weather conditions, but this is not really true. A skid does not just happen – it is almost always the result of a rider's actions. It is often caused by altering course or speed too harshly for the road conditions.

You should aim to ride and control a machine in such a way that it does not skid. This becomes more difficult when road or weather conditions deteriorate, but by using your skills of observation, anticipation and planning you can do a lot to minimise the risks of skidding.

First you need to understand how a skid happens, what warning signs to look out for and what actions to avoid.

How does a skid happen?

A machine skids when one or both tyres lose normal grip on the road, causing an involuntary movement of the machine. This happens when the grip of tyres on the road becomes less than the force or forces acting on the machine. The following illustrations explain what these forces are.

Accelerating

Braking

Cornering

These forces act on a machine whenever you operate the controls – the brakes, the throttle, the clutch or the handlebars. If you brake or accelerate while cornering, two forces are combined. As we saw in Chapter 4, there is only limited tyre grip available and if these forces become too powerful they break the grip of the tyres on the road. You should never ride to the limit of the tyre grip available – always leave a safety margin to allow for the unforeseen.

Skidding is usually the result of riding too fast for the conditions. This creates the circumstances from which a skid can develop. If a rider suddenly or forcibly accelerates, brakes, releases the clutch without matching engine speed to road speed or changes direction, this may cause loss of tyre grip. On a slippery road surface, it takes much less force to break the grip of the tyres.

If you have ever experienced a skid, you will probably remember that you were changing either the speed or direction of the machine – or both – just before the skid developed.

Causes of skidding

The commonest causes of skidding are:

- excessive speed for the circumstances
- coarse cornering at a speed which is not itself excessive
- excessive banking
- harsh acceleration
- sudden or excessive braking.

When a skid develops, the rider's first action should be to remove the cause. Later in this section we shall discuss the causes of skidding and how to remove them in more detail.

If you start to skid – remove the cause.

Minimising the risks of skidding

A clear understanding of the causes of skidding should help you to plan to avoid skidding in the first place. In Chapter 3 we talked about the importance of observation, anticipation and planning as the skills which are essential to safe riding and smooth progress. How can you apply these skills to reduce the risks of skidding?

Observe – weather and road conditions to watch out for

Skidding is more likely in bad weather conditions and on slippery road surfaces. These are some of the obvious and less obvious hazards you need to watch out for:

- snow, ice, frost, heavy rain
- wet mud or damp leaves, which can create sudden slippery patches on the road surface
- cold spots in shaded areas, under trees, on slopes or hills, ie micro climates – watch how other vehicles behave in icy weather
- a shower or rain after a long dry spell – accumulated rubber

dust and oil mixed with water can create a very slippery surface

- dry loose dust or gravel
- oil, diesel or fuel oil spillages – common at junctions, roundabouts and service stations
- worn road surfaces that have become polished smooth
- metal grills and covers, cat's eyes, tar banding and road paint, especially when wet
- concrete, which usually provides good grip, but which may hold surface water and become slippery in freezing weather
- road surfaced with setts or cobbles – still found in some towns and cities and can be very slippery when wet
- ice and other changes of the road surface on bridges – may be more slippery than the surrounding roads.

The risks of these hazards are accentuated at corners and junctions because you are more likely to combine braking, accelerating and turning in these situations.

Anticipate and plan – adjust your riding to the road conditions

Good road observation will enable you to evaluate poor weather and road conditions accurately and adjust your speed accordingly.

- Leave plenty of room for manoeuvres, reduce your speed and increase the distance you allow for stopping to match the road conditions – on a slippery surface a machine can take many times the normal distance to stop.
- Use the throttle and a lower gear to reduce speed on a slippery road. It is essential that any gear change is accompanied by a smooth matching of engine speed to road speed.
- Use a higher gear in slippery conditions to avoid wheel spin, especially when moving off or travelling at low speeds.
- On a slippery surface aim to brake, change gear and corner as smoothly as possible, so that the grip of the tyres is not broken.

Care of the machine

Most skids are the result of how a machine is ridden, but keeping your machine and tyres in good condition helps to minimise the risk of skidding:

- tyres should be correctly inflated and have adequate tread depth – check tyre treads and tyre pressure daily
- defective brakes and faulty suspension are especially dangerous on slippery surfaces and may help to cause or aggravate a skid – do not increase the risk by neglecting these problems.

Recognising and removing the cause of a skid

If your machine develops a full skid you are unlikely to have the time and space to correct it. You need full concentration and observation both to avoid skids and to be able to take immediate corrective action if one starts to develop.

When a skid develops, the first action should be to recognise what type it is and remove the cause.

Rear wheel skid

This occurs when the rear wheel loses its grip because of:

- excessive speed for the circumstances
- excessive banking during cornering
- harsh acceleration
- excessive braking
- not matching engine speed to road speed when releasing the clutch.

A rear wheel skid can cause the rear wheel to slide to either side. During cornering, the wheel will swing to the outside of the curve. The machine may turn broadside and go completely out of control. It may fall to the inside of the curve if the machine is banked.

Remove the cause by easing off the throttle or reducing braking effort and bring the machine upright. Steer in the direction of the skid. When stability is restored, apply the throttle or brake but with greater sensitivity than before.

Of the two types of skid a rear wheel skid is the more controllable.

Front wheel skid

This occurs when the front wheel loses its grip because of:

- excessive speed for the circumstances
- excessive turn on the handlebars
- excessive banking during cornering
- excessive braking.

If you have the time and space, remove the cause of a front wheel skid. There is very little time to recognise, react to and correct a front wheel skid, so make every effort to avoid one.

If the machine is banked and the front wheel suddenly regains its grip the machine will be unbalanced, on the wrong course and in danger of falling to the outside of the curve. Restore control by returning the machine to an upright position and reducing speed.

Aquaplaning

One of the most frightening experiences a rider can have is aquaplaning. This is where a wedge of water builds up between the front tyre and the road surface, often because of an inadequate depth of tyre tread. Whether you brake or steer the machine will not respond. The safest solution is to maintain a firm hold on the handlebars and gradually close the throttle, allowing the machine to lose speed and the tyres to regain their grip.

Never practise skidding on a public road.

Analyse your own experience of skidding

Now that you have a fuller understanding of what causes a skid, think back over your riding career and recall any skids you have had. For each skid you can remember ask yourself :

What were the causes of the skid?

What type of skid was it?

Could you have anticipated these conditions and avoided the skid altogether?

Did you manage to quickly regain directional control? If not, how could you have improved your handling of the skid?

How have you changed your riding as a result of the experience? Has reading this chapter made you aware of further changes that you need to make?

Review

In this chapter we have looked at:

- the four principles of safe cornering
- the forces acting on a bike on bends and corners
- why motorcycles are less stable when cornering
- the characteristics that affect a machine's ability to corner
- how camber affects the ability to corner
- the use of the system of motorcycle control for cornering
- the technique of limit point analysis
- how to position yourself on the approach to a bend
- how to reduce the curvature of a bend
- how to assess the speed for a bend.
- how a rider's actions can cause a skid
- how to reduce the risks of skidding
- front wheel and rear wheel skids and how to correct them
- how ABS, linked braking and traction control work.

Check your understanding

What are the four principles of safe cornering?

Why are bikes less stable when cornering?

Why are you less able to steer if you brake or accelerate sharply?

In which direction do you go if tyre grip is lost on a right-hand bend?

Why is the fall of the camber an important consideration during cornering?

What is meant by the limit point and how do you use it to corner safely?

Explain where to position your bike during cornering, taking account of safety, observation and reducing the curvature of the bend.

What are the causes of skidding?

How do you avoid skidding?

If you have difficulty in answering any of these questions, look back over the relevant part of this chapter to refresh your memory.

Use this chapter to find out:

- the purpose of signals
- the range of signals available to you
- how to avoid confusion
- when to use arm signals
- why courtesy signals are important.

Chapter 6

Signals

Developing your skill at using signals

Using signals may seem to be a basic skill, but many riders do not use their signals consistently, and do not know how to make the most effective use of the full range of signals available to them. This chapter will help you to identify areas in which your skill at using signals can be developed and improved.

See Chapter 2, The system of motorcycle control, page 30, The importance of the information phase.

Skill in using your signals is an important element in applying the system of motorcycle control. Signalling is one of the key ways in which we give information to other road users, and giving information is a key part of the information phase of the system.

The purpose of signals

The purpose of signals is to inform other road users of your presence or intentions. You should give a signal whenever it could benefit other road users, but do not signal indiscriminately.

Only give a signal when another road user may benefit from it.

Signals are used to give information, so they must be given clearly, in good time and in accordance with the methods illustrated in the *Highway Code*. As with any communication, signals can easily be misinterpreted. Always make the meaning of your signals clear. Other road users use your position and speed to interpret what your signals mean, so be aware of this, especially when safety or other considerations cause you to take an unusual position. These are the key points to remember:

- consider the need to give a signal on the approach to every hazard, and before you change direction or speed

- give a signal whenever it could benefit other road users
- remember that signalling does not give you any right to carry out the actions you indicate
- follow the *Highway Code* – carry out rear observation before you signal or manoeuvre.

Avoid confusion

As well as taking care that your own signals are not misleading, you also need to be cautious about how you interpret the signals of others. For example, does a vehicle flashing the left-hand indicator mean that the driver intends to:

- park the vehicle, possibly immediately after a left-hand junction?
- turn into a left-hand junction?
- carry straight on, having forgotten to cancel the last signal?

In practice you should use the position and speed of the vehicle to interpret the intentions of the driver.

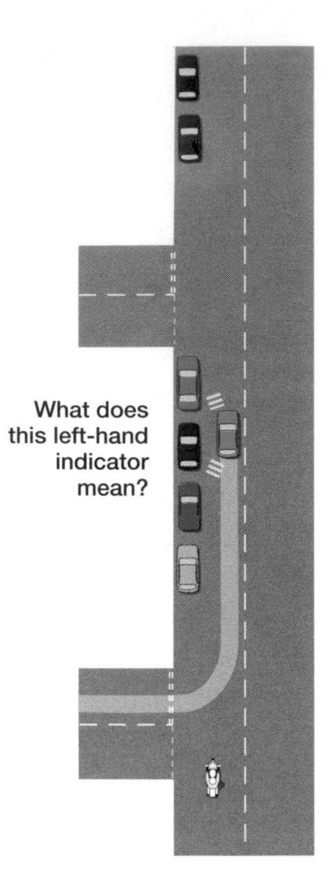

> Do you trust the signals of other road users or do you wait for some other confirmation of their intentions?

The range of signals

The signals available to you are:

- indicators
- horn signals
- hazard warning lights
- brakelights
- headlight
- arm signals
- courtesy signals.

Below we look at how you can make best use of these signals, each of which has its advantages and disadvantages. Where there is a choice, always consider which signal is likely to be the most effective.

Using the indicators

The indicators on some low-powered machines are not very effective because the lamps are of relatively low wattage. This is especially true when direct sunlight shines on their lenses. Check that the indicator lamps on the machines you use are sufficiently brilliant to attract the attention of other road users. If they are not, consider using arm signals instead.

The system of motorcycle control advises you to give a signal only when pedestrians or other road users could benefit. This helps your riding because:

- it encourages you to be attentive and aware of what is happening on the road around you, especially behind you
- it reduces the number of hand movements you have to make
- it reduces signalling clutter; there is always the possibility that your signal could be misinterpreted.

Remember that road users who could benefit include those in front as well as those behind.

If you decide signalling is appropriate you should give a signal for each manoeuvre you intend to carry out. One signal should not cover two manoeuvres. Use your indicators in accordance with the *Highway Code*, but bear in mind the following points.

- A signal to indicate that you are going to turn left and a signal to indicate that you intend to pull into the side of the road and stop can easily be confused by other road users. If there is a possibility of causing confusion, take steps to avoid it. Consider giving an arm signal to clarify your intentions. Be particularly careful if you intend to park just past a left-hand junction, especially if a vehicle is waiting to emerge.
- Use your position to make your intentions clear to other road users. If you cannot use your road position, or if you think it necessary, reinforce your indicator signal with an arm signal. For example, you indicate to turn right but a parked vehicle causes you to move to the centre of the road just before the junction. Other drivers may think you have indicated to warn

of your intention to move out to pass the parked vehicle. Adding an arm signal makes it clear that you intend to turn right.

Cancelling indicator signals

Leaving an indicator working after making a turn confuses other drivers and can easily cause an accident. Do not accept an indicator signal as complete proof of another driver's intention when you are waiting to emerge from a side turning. Look for supporting evidence such as an obvious slowing down before you move out.

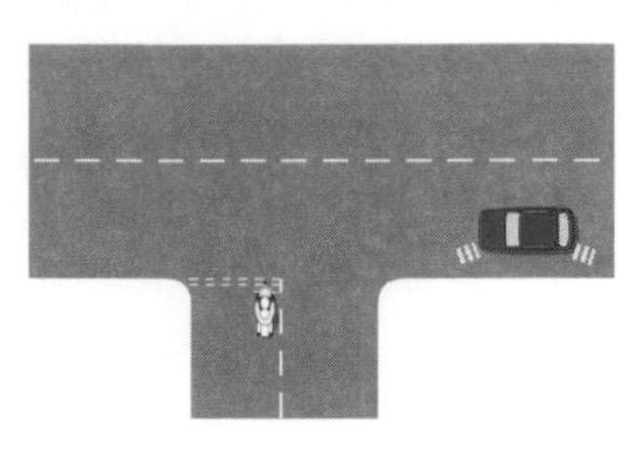

At present, some machines do not have indicator self-cancelling mechanisms. Always make sure you cancel a signal immediately after you have completed the manoeuvre.

Some machines are fitted with a self-cancelling mechanism that is activated by either the distance travelled or the time that has elapsed, depending on the speed of the bike. If your machine has a self-cancelling system you must know how it works. Read the manufacturer's manual.

These mechanisms can cancel themselves when they are still needed, for example, when going round a large roundabout. Be alert to this possibility and be ready to switch the indicator back on.

Over the next week monitor how you use indicator signals.

Do you only use them when someone else could benefit?

Do you always use them clearly?

Do you ever use an arm signal?

Do you take care to cancel them promptly?

Identify areas where your use of indicator signals could be improved. Work out what changes you need to make, and decide how and when you will apply them.

Using the horn

The horns on some machines are ineffective because of their low power. Sound levels that seem adequate to riders may go unnoticed by drivers cocooned in their vehicles. Satisfy yourself that the horn on any machine you ride is effective in traffic conditions before you regard it as a satisfactory signalling aid.

Sound your horn when it could benefit pedestrians or other road users in situations where they may not have noticed you or cannot see you.

You should consider using the horn on the approach to any hazard. When you decide it is necessary to sound the horn, alter your position or speed so that you can stop if there is no reaction to your warning. Do not use the horn to challenge or rebuke other road users. Be aware that some people, especially children, the elderly and those with a hearing disability may not hear a horn.

These are the key points to remember:

- first alter your position to avoid the hazard and consider reducing your speed, then sound the horn to inform the other road user(s)
- use your horn in good time
- adjust the length of the horn note to the circumstances
- using the horn does not justify using excessive speed for the circumstances (for example, when riding round a blind bend)
- listen carefully for other road users' horn warnings and react appropriately – remember horns can be difficult to hear with a helmet on.

How do you use the horn? Do you use it to help other road users or do you use it as a last resort?

Over the next day or two notice how many times you hear the horn used to assist other drivers, and how many times it is used to rebuke them.

These are examples of circumstances where it could be beneficial to use the horn:

to attract the attention of another road user who is obviously vulnerable (pedestrians and cyclists – especially children – are most at risk)

to inform the driver in front of your presence before you overtake

when you approach a hazard where the view is very limited – for example, a blind bend or hump-back bridge

to warn the occupants of parked vehicles that you are about to pass them.

Using hazard warning lights

Only use hazard lights to alert other drivers to your presence when you have stopped. Do not use hazard lights when moving except on unrestricted dual carriageways and motorways. Here you can use hazard lights briefly to warn the vehicles behind that there is a hold-up.

Using the brakelight

Use the brakelight to indicate that you are slowing down or intend to stop. Remember to carry out rear observation before using your brakes.

- Use your brakelight as an early indication of your intention to slow down. Lightly touch your brakes, well in advance of the anticipated hazard, to alert the driver behind to your intention. This is especially useful when the driver behind is too close.
- Remember that rear foglights are as bright as brakelights and may mask them when you are slowing down.

Flashing your headlight

Use headlight flashes when the horn would not be heard, and in place of the horn at night. Headlight flashes should only be used for one purpose: to inform other road users of your presence. Never assume that a headlight flash from another driver is a signal to proceed. Be aware that some drivers may interpret a headlight flash as an act of aggression.

A headlight flash can be used before overtaking in daylight to alert other drivers to your presence. Flash your headlight early enough to allow the other drivers to react to it. When and for how long to give the flash is a matter of fine judgement. It depends on your speed and the road and traffic conditions. The purpose of the flash is to inform the drivers in front of your presence, not that you intend to overtake. It does not give you the right to overtake. Use it when speed makes it likely that the horn would not be heard.

During darkness use headlight flashes to inform other road users of your presence:

- on the approach to a hill crest or narrow hump-back bridge
- when travelling along very narrow, winding roads.

Do not give these signals when they might be misunderstood by road users for whom they are not intended.

Using arm signals

You should be able to give arm signals in accordance with the *Highway Code* and understand what they mean.

Riders generally make more use of arm signals than drivers. This is because some machines do not have indicators and others have indicators of such low power that they are ineffective.

The advantages of arm signals are that they:

- are free from mechanical failure
- cannot be left on
- attract attention because they break the outline of machine and rider
- can be seen from the front of the machine when used for slowing-down signals
- are clearly distinguishable in bright sunlight, when indicator lenses may not be
- can be used to confirm the rider's intention.

Common situations where arm signals could be useful to reinforce another signal are:

to reinforce a right-hand turn indicator in an unclear situation

to reinforce brakelights on the approach to a pedestrian crossing.

Do not use arm signals when you need both hands on the handlebars to control the machine, such as during heavy braking at speed or sharp cornering. Remember that releasing the throttle to make a right arm signal can dramatically reduce the speed of the machine.

Using courtesy signals

Courtesy signals are important because they encourage cooperative use of the roadspace and promote road safety. Acknowledging the courtesy of other road users encourages good motorcycling and helps you to develop a positive attitude to riding. Using a courtesy signal to apologise or defuse a potential conflict can make a real difference to road safety. Use courtesy signals:

- to thank other road users for giving you priority
- to apologise when you have unintentionally caused inconvenience.

In most cases nodding your head is a safe and sufficient way to acknowledge a courtesy. If you use a hand use the left, but not at the risk of losing control of the machine. Make sure your courtesy signal could not be mistaken by other road users as an instruction to stop or to pull over to the side.

Responding to other people's signals

Signals other than those given by authorised persons should be treated with caution. If someone beckons you to move forward, always check for yourself whether it is safe to do so.

On your route home from work, aim to increase the number of courtesy signals that you give and acknowledge (providing it is safe to do so).

How does this affect your state of mind?

Does it influence the actions of other drivers?

If you find you are reluctant to increase the number of courtesy signals you give, ask yourself why. What does this say about your attitudes to your own riding and to other road users?

Review

In this chapter we have looked at:

- the place of signals in the system of motorcycle control
- why it is important to give signals clearly
- the different signals available to you, and how and when to use them
- how courtesy signals can contribute to road safety.

Check your understanding

When should you consider signalling?

What should you do before you signal or manoeuvre?

Why must you take care in interpreting the signals of other road users?

Why should you only signal when someone else could benefit?

Why do left-hand junctions pose problems for interpreting indicator signals?

In what circumstances should hazard warning lights be used?

What are the guidelines for using the horn?

Explain why you might use arm signals to reinforce other signals.

How do courtesy signals contribute to road safety?

If you have difficulty in answering any of these questions, look back over the relevant part of this chapter to refresh your memory.

Use this chapter to find out:

- where to position your bike on the road
- which hazards to look for
- how to improve your views
- how to choose a position for following vehicles
- how to position your bike for bends and corners.

Chapter 7

Positioning

Developing your skill at positioning your bike

Positioning is a crucial element in the system of motorcycle control. This chapter looks at the key factors that you need to consider when deciding how to position your bike in different circumstances.

See Chapter 2, The system of motorcycle control.

The ideal road position depends on many things: safety, observation, road and traffic conditions, road layout, cornering, manoeuvrability, assisting traffic flow and making your intentions clear. The overriding consideration is safety, which should never be sacrificed for any other advantage. As far as there is a standard position on the road, it is one which gives priority to safety, which ensures good tyre grip and stability and which provides the best view consistent with these objectives.

When choosing your road position never sacrifice safety for any other advantage.

Position is critical to safety. By carefully choosing your position you can do much to reduce the risk of having an accident. The diagram at the top of page 117 shows how you can think of the road as zones of different risk.

Zones of different risk

To the nearside there is a risk of coming into conflict with emerging vehicles, cyclists and pedestrians (especially children), and parked vehicles and their occupants.

To the offside, there is a risk of coming into conflict with oncoming vehicles and vehicles crossing from the offside.

Between these two extremes there is a relatively safe zone. This is towards the left of the centre of the road, giving sufficient clearance to pedestrians and other nearside hazards.

This is only a very general area of safety and you must adapt your position to the actual circumstances.

Positioning for advantage

The narrowness of rider and machine gives you great flexibility in the choice of position on your own side of the road. Choose a position to maximise safety. There are three positions to consider.

The nearside position

The benefits of this position are:

- it gives early views through right-hand bends
- it allows nearside views past lorries and other large vehicles
- it allows extra space for oncoming vehicles
- it is generally the best position for left-hand turns when there are no other hazards.

Check that the nearside road surface is sound and free of drains, debris, dust and grit before using it.

The central position

This is midway between the better part of the nearside edge and the centre line.

The benefits of this position are:

- it gives the rider good margins of safety on both sides
- it allows the rider to change position to either side.

In wet weather, avoid the central position near junctions and on the final approach to bends, because oil and diesel tend to accumulate in it.

The offside position

The benefits of this position are:

- it gives early views on the approach to left-hand bends
- it provides increased safety margins away from nearside hazards
- it is generally the best position for right turns.

Anticipate the possibility of large oncoming vehicles straddling the central line on bends and be prepared to move to the left.

Any of these positions should be sacrificed for safety.

When you are riding through a series of bends in wet weather follow the dry line of previous vehicles providing it does not take you too far off course. Reduce speed to compensate for deviating from your ideal line.

Positioning on the approach to hazards

The system of motorcycle control provides a safe and methodical approach to hazards. Part of this approach is an awareness of the likely risks involved. This section describes the factors you should take into account as you position your machine to approach and pass hazards.

As you approach a hazard you need to be aware of the condition of the road surface up to and through the hazard, and to select a course that will give you adequate tyre grip. When planning your course be alert to risks that arise from the sides of the road. Dangers can come from anywhere but you will generally have less time to react to hazards coming from the nearside. In narrow roads and one-way systems you need to be equally attentive to both sides of the road. Select a course that reduces your vulnerability and increases your vision and conspicuousness.

Roadside hazards

Common roadside hazards that you should be aware of are:

- pedestrians, especially children, stepping off the footpath
- parked vehicles and their occupants
- cyclists, especially children
- concealed junctions
- animals.

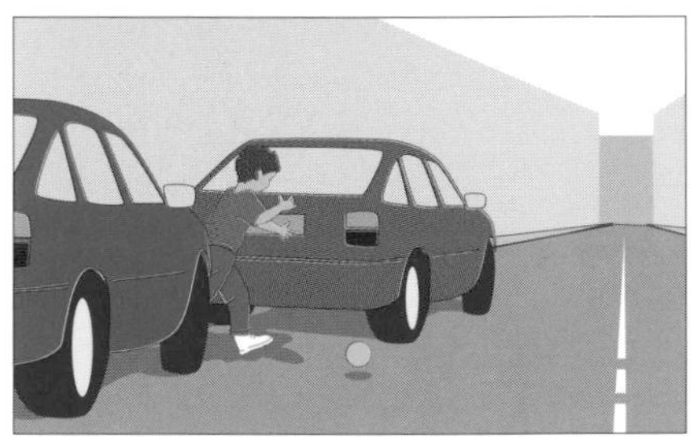

If you identify hazards on the nearside, select a course closer to the crown of the road. This has two benefits:

- it gives you a better view
- it provides more space in which to take avoiding action should this become necessary.

If oncoming traffic makes it unsafe to adopt this position, or if the road is too narrow, reduce your speed. There is an important trade-off between your speed and the clearance around your machine. **The less space you have the slower you should go**.

One-third of children involved in road accidents did not look first.

When you ride along a row of parked vehicles get into the habit of asking yourself, 'Could I stop in time if a child ran out?'

Keep as far from rows of parked vehicles as circumstances allow. There is always the possibility that a pedestrian, especially a child, might run out from between them, or that an occupant might suddenly step out into your path. If traffic or road conditions prevent you from moving out, slow down. A good rule of thumb is to try to give at least an open door's clearance to the side of any parked vehicles.

Improving the view into nearside road junctions

Position yourself so that you can see as much of the road ahead as possible and so that other road users can see you. You can improve your view into nearside roads by positioning your bike towards the crown of the road. This also makes you more visible to vehicles pulling out from nearside junctions. You must take into account any vehicles on your offside before you change position, and the possibility that bikes or vehicles may move up on your inside if you do. Adopt a position that minimises the overall danger from both sides of the road. Carry out rear observation before you alter position either way.

Position to see and be seen.

Review your skill at positioning for safety

On your next journey, monitor your road positioning from the viewpoint of safety.

Do you pay enough attention to:
- nearside hazards?
- offside hazards?

Do you position your bike to obtain the best view in the circumstances, with due regard to safety?

Are there ways in which you could improve your positioning in order to increase safety?

Following position

In a stream of traffic, always keep a safe distance behind the vehicle in front. A guide for following distances in open conditions is one metre/yard per mph between you and the vehicle in front. See the section on stopping distances in the *Highway Code*.

*See Chapter 4, **Acceleration, using gears and braking**, page 82, **The two-second rule**.*

Always try to maintain a view of the road beyond the vehicles you are following. These are some of the advantages of keeping your distance from the vehicle in front:

- you have a good view, and can increase it along both sides by slight changes of position – this enables you to be fully aware of what is happening on the road ahead
- you can stop your machine safely if the driver in front brakes firmly without warning
- you can extend your braking distance so that the driver behind has more time to react
- you suffer less from the spray from the vehicle in front in wet weather
- you can see when it is safe to move up into the overtaking position.

You should generally position your machine to the rear offside of the vehicle you are following. From this position you are:

- visible through the inside and offside door mirrors of the driver in front
- able to move into an overtaking position by reducing the following distance alone (without needing to change position as well)
- able to escape to either side should an emergency arise.

If you need to take a position further to the centre or nearside, increase your following distance to compensate for the loss of the offside escape route.

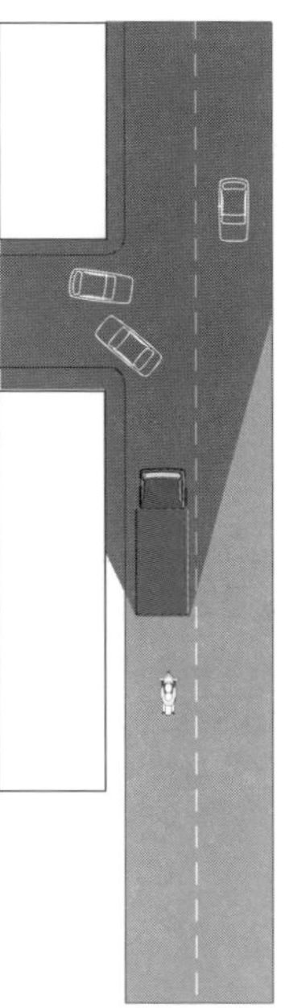

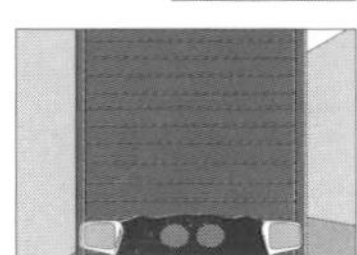

In this illustration the rider is following too closely to the vehicle in front. The aerial plan shows how hazards in the shaded area cannot be seen.

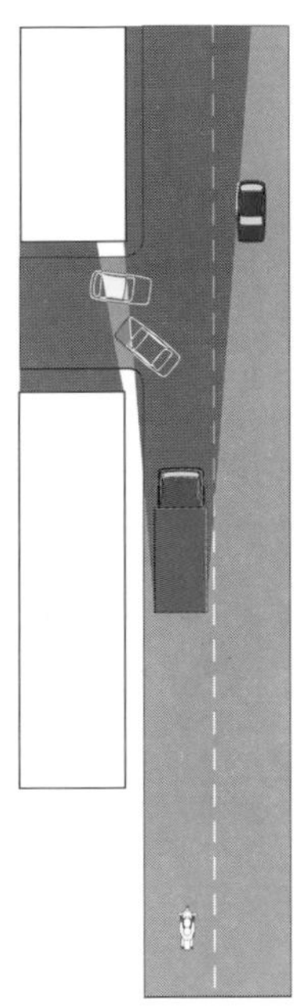

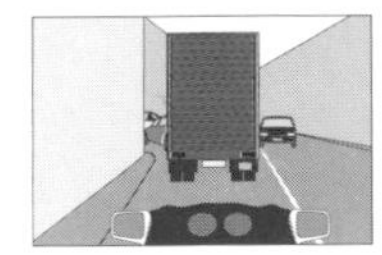

In this illustration the rider is keeping a good safe position and all the hazards are visible. This view could be improved by moving slightly to the nearside or offside.

> Over the last month have you had to brake severely to avoid running into a vehicle in front?
>
> If this has happened more than once, were the situations similar?
>
> How have you altered your riding behaviour to prevent this happening again?

Overtaking position

See Chapter 8, **Overtaking**, page 131, **Stage two: the overtaking position**.

When you have identified an opportunity to overtake, you should move into the overtaking position. This is closer to the vehicle in front than the following position and you should only use it in readiness for overtaking. If an observed or anticipated hazard comes into view consider moving back to your normal following position.

As you move closer to the vehicle in front the driver is likely to realise that you want to overtake. You must be careful not to intimidate the driver or to appear aggressive by following too closely. Such misunderstandings are dangerous and counter-productive. They can cause the other driver either to speed up, making it more difficult to overtake, or to brake unexpectedly at a point where your safety margin is reduced.

Position for turning

Your position for turning depends on the other traffic, your safety, road surface conditions, the road layout, the position of any obstacles and the effect of these obstacles on traffic behaviour. Generally, the best position to approach the junction where you are going to turn is on the nearside for a left turn and towards the centre line for a right turn.

Give careful consideration to:

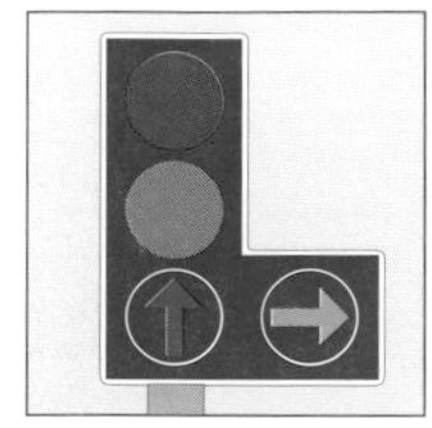

traffic light filter arrows

carriageway markings

other traffic

obstructions.

If you intend to turn right and oncoming traffic is encroaching on your side of the road, move away from the centre line.

If you intend to turn left and the corner has a sharp angle, or is obscured, or pedestrians are present, approach the corner from further out than you normally would. Avoid 'swan necking', which is approaching close to the nearside and then swinging out to the right just before turning left into the junction.

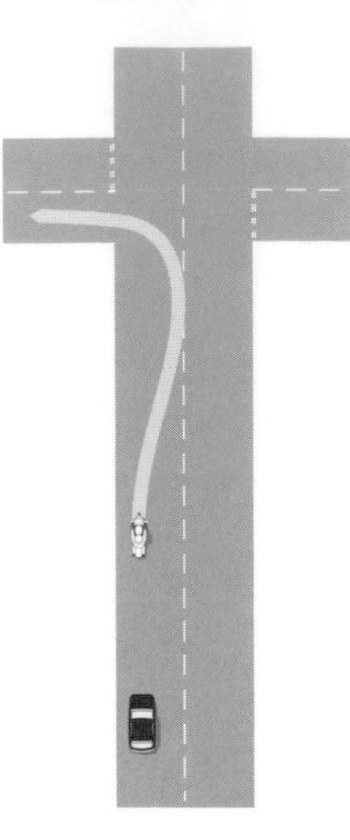

Avoid approaching close to the nearside and then swinging out to the right before turning left – 'swan necking'.

Crossroads

The *Highway Code* advises that two vehicles turning across each other at a crossroads should pass each other offside to offside. But where traffic conditions, the junction layout or local practice makes this impractical, pass nearside to nearside. Take extra care while doing this because the other vehicle conceals your presence from oncoming traffic and obstructs your view of the road. Look carefully for oncoming traffic. Riders are extremely vulnerable when carrying out this manoeuvre.

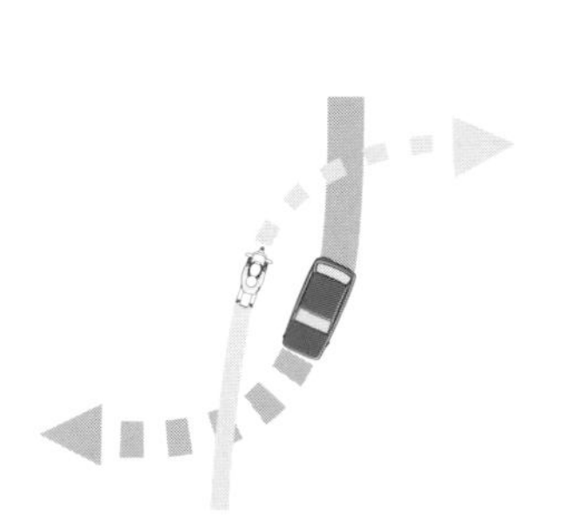

Passing offside to offside

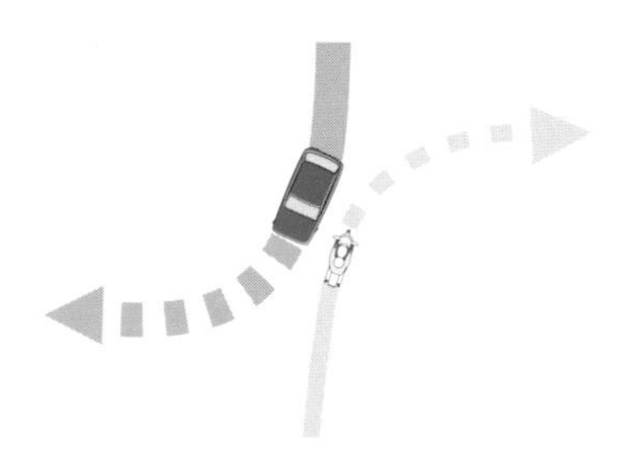

Passing nearside to nearside

Take extra care on a nearside to nearside pass because your view of the road is obstructed by the other vehicle. Look carefully for oncoming traffic.

Position for stopping behind other vehicles

Before you come to a stop think about your next move. Position your bike so that you can continue with minimum inconvenience to yourself and other road users.

Leave yourself sufficient room to pull out and pass the vehicle in front if necessary.

When you stop behind a line of vehicles and there is no one following, consider stopping well short of the vehicle in front and watch for traffic coming up behind. If an approaching vehicle appears to have left braking too late, move forward to allow it extra space to stop in. An example of this is where there are traffic lights at a roadworks close to a bend. You should consider stopping in the bend so that the drivers of following vehicles can see you as they approach the bend.

Parking

Park your bike safely, preferably on level firm ground, away from strong winds and on its central stand: do not leave it where it can cause inconvenience or danger to others. If you park on a hill, face the bike uphill, put it in first gear and use the side stand. Consider angling the rear wheel into the kerb.

Never sit on the bike to move it off its central stand. The stand is not designed to take the combined weight of you and the machine.

Review

In this chapter we have looked at:

- the overriding importance of safety in choosing a road position
- the relative merits of different positions
- common roadside hazards that you need to be aware of
- where to position your bike when hazards are present
- where to position your bike while following a vehicle in front
- how to position your machine for turning and stopping
- how to turn past another vehicle at a crossroads.

Check your understanding

What is the overriding factor in determining your road position?

List the common nearside and offside risks that you should take into account when deciding on your position.

If you ride down a road where the space to the sides is restricted, what should you do?

How much clearance should you generally give parked vehicles?

How can you improve your view into nearside junctions?

What are the advantages of keeping your distance from the vehicle in front?

How should you approach a left-hand junction when pedestrians are present?

Why do you need to be careful if you pass nearside to nearside at a junction?

If you have difficulty in answering any of these questions, look back over the relevant part of this chapter to refresh your memory.

Use this chapter to find out:

- how to overtake safely
- how to pass stationary vehicles
- how to overtake moving vehicles
- which special hazards you need to consider before overtaking
- how to filter safely
- how to assist other drivers to overtake.

Chapter 8

Overtaking

Developing your skill at overtaking safely

This chapter explains how to use the system of motorcycle control to overtake and identifies the additional hazards that you need to consider to carry out the manoeuvre safely.

The high viewing position, manoeuvrability and rapid acceleration of motorcycles give them great advantages in overtaking. These, together with their narrow roadspace requirements, should make them the safest of all vehicles on which to overtake. The fact that they are not is because riders fail to appreciate all the hazards involved.

Overtaking is hazardous because it may bring you into the path of other vehicles. It is a complex manoeuvre in which you need to consider a number of subsidiary hazards as well as the primary hazard presented by the vehicle(s) to be overtaken. Applying the system of motorcycle control enables you carry out the manoeuvre safely.

Key safety points

When you are considering overtaking, always follow this safety advice:

- do not overtake where you cannot see far enough ahead to be sure it is safe
- avoid causing other vehicles (overtaken, following or approaching) to alter course or speed
- always be able to move back to the nearside in plenty of time
- always be ready to abandon overtaking if a new hazard comes into view
- do not overtake in situations where you might come into

conflict with other road users (these are identified in the overtaking section of the *Highway Code*)

- avoid making a third line of vehicles abreast wherever possible
- never overtake on the nearside on dual carriageways and motorways except in slow-moving queues of traffic when filtering or when offside queues are moving more slowly
- be aware of the potential dangers when filtering.

Remember that overtaking is your decision and you can reconsider it at any point.

Overtaking places you in a zone of potential danger, and requires good judgement if it is to be safe. The ability to overtake with consistent safety only comes with experience and practice. Even when you have acquired this skill you need to be extremely cautious. Always be patient and leave a margin of safety to allow for errors. **If in doubt hold back**.

Practise applying the key safety points

Write out the eight points of the overtaking safety advice listed above. (If you cannot recall the *Highway Code* advice obtain a current edition and refresh your memory.) Take your list with you the next time you ride and monitor how well you follow the advice in the relevant situations. When you get an opportunity for a break, go through the list and mark the points that you failed to consider or comply with fully.

Work out why you did not follow the advice and plan a way of improving your future performance. Note this down and review your performance again in a fortnight.

Passing stationary vehicles

Passing stationary vehicles is relatively straightforward. Use the system to approach and assess the hazard, and to pass it with safety. Take account of the position and speed of oncoming traffic, the position and speed of following traffic and the presence of pedestrians. If the situation allows, keep at least a door's width away from the side of the stationary vehicle.

Overtaking moving vehicles

Overtaking a moving vehicle is complicated because the hazards are moving and the situation changes all the time. You need to consider the speed and acceleration capabilities of your own machine, and the relative speeds of other vehicles. You also need to be able to predict where vehicles and gaps in the traffic will converge. To do this safely requires careful observation and planning, good judgement of speed and distance, and an awareness of the many possible secondary hazards.

How to overtake

When you are catching up with another vehicle you should decide whether to adjust your speed and follow while it makes reasonable progress, or to overtake at the first safe opportunity. Whatever your decision, careful use of acceleration sense will assist the ease and smoothness of your manoeuvre. If you decide to overtake, assess whether you can approach and overtake in one continuous manoeuvre, or whether you will have to follow for a while until a suitable opportunity arises. Either way, the vehicle in front is a hazard so you need to consider the various phases of the system to deal with it safely.

You will meet other road users besides vehicles, and you need to consider their special needs. Avoid startling horses. Be aware that cyclists, especially children, can be erratic and allow them plenty of room.

The following pages explain how to use the system of motorcycle control to tackle the two overtaking situations we have identified:

- **when the absence of other hazards allows you to approach and overtake in one manoeuvre**

- **when other hazards require you to take up a following position before you can overtake.**

In real life both these situations may of course develop and become complicated by further hazards, but for the moment our main concern is to explain the two different methods as clearly as possible. The additional hazards you need to consider are identified later in the chapter.

Overtaking in the absence of additional hazards

You have identified that there is only one hazard present – the vehicle ahead that you are gaining on – and all the other conditions (such as clear view, sufficient space and absence of oncoming traffic) are suitable for immediate overtaking. Take the decision to overtake and work through the stages of the system to pass the slower vehicle(s) in one smooth manoeuvre.

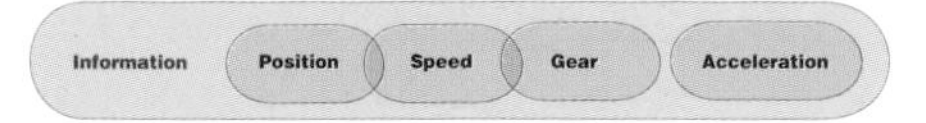

Information

Observe the road ahead for road signs and markings, layout, approaching vehicles, other hazards, and any obstructed views which could conceal hazards. Identify a safe return gap. Observe the speed and position of any vehicles behind you, make sure you know what is in your blind spot. Judge the relative speeds of your own machine and the vehicle(s) to be overtaken. Plan your overtaking manoeuvre. Consider a lifesaver check and a signal: carry them out if appropriate.

Position

At the appropriate point, take a course to overtake the vehicle ahead.

Speed

Adjust your speed to complete the manoeuvre within the road space you know to be clear, and before any approaching vehicle could come into conflict with you.

Gear

Select the most responsive gear for the speed.

Acceleration

Adjust your speed to return to the identified gap, and continue with your journey.

Overtaking when other hazards require you to take up a following position

This occurs when the presence of approaching vehicles, obscured views or some other hazard requires you to follow the vehicle(s) ahead before you can overtake safely. Overtaking in this situation requires a three-stage approach as illustrated on the right.

Stage 3
overtaking

Stage 2
the overtaking position

Stage 1
the following position

Stage one: the following position

Where you are gaining on a vehicle in front, and it is not possible to overtake immediately, use the system of motorcycle control to reduce your speed to that of the vehicle in front to follow at a safe distance.

Your main task in the following position is to observe and assess the road and traffic conditions for an opportunity to overtake safely. You need to ask yourself:

Observe what is happening in the far distance, the middle ground, the immediate foreground and behind; do this repeatedly and look in the mirror frequently.

Your safety depends on making the correct interpretation of what you see. It is not enough just to see it.

In some circumstances it may be possible, as you close up on a vehicle in front, to miss out stage one and go straight to stage two: the overtaking position. This is determined by your view of the road ahead and whether any additional hazards are present that would make the overtaking position unsafe. If you do go straight to the overtaking position, you still need to observe and assess the hazards identified in the diagram.

Stage two: the overtaking position

The overtaking position is usually closer than the following position and minimises the distance you have to travel to overtake. It can also indicate to the driver in front that you wish to overtake. Adopt this position so that you are ready to overtake when a safe opportunity arises.

Because it is closer than the following position you have less time to react to the actions of the vehicle in front, so you must be sure that there are no hazards ahead which might cause it to brake suddenly. You can only know this if you have been able to fully observe the road ahead.

Work through the stages of the system to move up to the overtaking position.

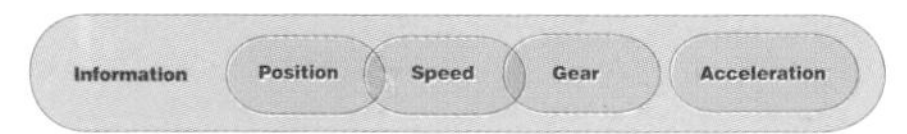

Information

Observe the road ahead, behind and to the side for an opportunity to safely occupy the overtaking position. Take into account hazards that can be seen and the possible dangers in areas that cannot be seen. Plan your move when you see an opportunity developing. Remember the need for rear observation if you do not know what is in your blind spot. Consider the need to signal.

Position

Move up to the overtaking position. This is the closest position to the vehicle in front that is consistent with the hazards and that gives an adequate view of the road ahead. It is not possible to define this position exactly: it depends on an awareness of the possible dangers, good judgement and experience.

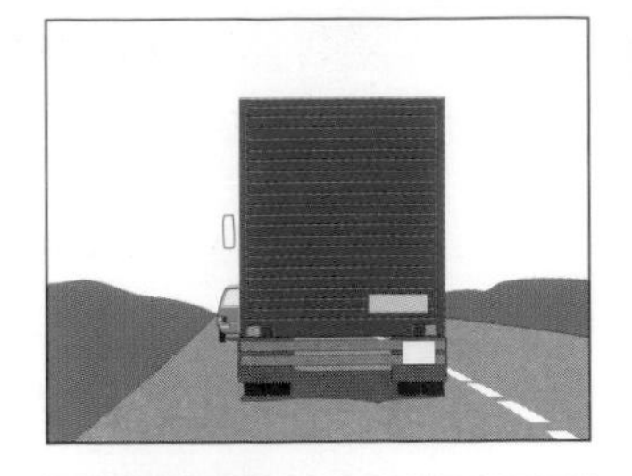

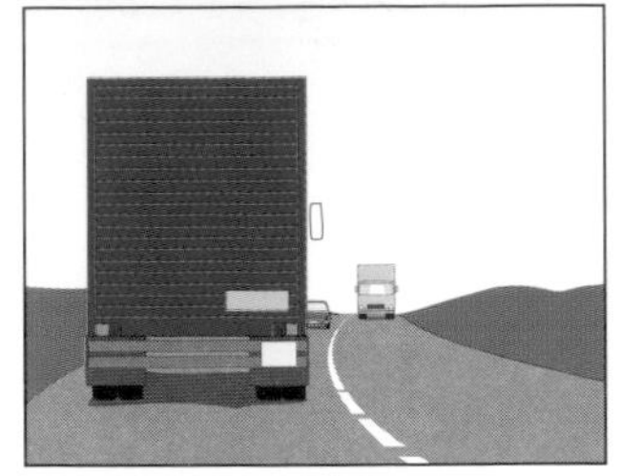

With large vehicles and where it helps, take a view along both sides of the vehicle.

Take views to the offside, nearside, through the windows and under and over the vehicle in front. Generally position your machine towards the offside rear corner of the vehicle in front. This position has two advantages:

- the driver in front can see you through the interior mirror and the side mirror
- you have an escape route to the offside.

Avoid sitting in the blind spot of any vehicles you intend to overtake. Be aware that the closer you get to the vehicle in front the more likely you are to intimidate the driver.

The larger the vehicle in front, the further back you need to be.

Speed

Adjust your speed to that of the vehicle in front.

Gear

If you are not already in an appropriate gear, select the most responsive gear for the speed, bearing in mind that this is the gear you will use to accelerate as you overtake. Do not choose too low a gear in an attempt to avoid braking when you return to the nearside after overtaking. Good observation, judgement and acceleration sense should enable you to return to the nearside without braking.

As the overtaking position is closer than the following position you must observe carefully for any new hazards. If a hazard comes into sight, consider dropping back to the following position until the hazard is passed. When planning to overtake you need to know exactly what is on the road ahead and to be aware of the possible pitfalls. Observation, planning, judgement of speed and distance and attention to detail are crucial. Thoughtless overtaking is dangerous.

Stage three: overtaking

From the overtaking position continue observing until you identify an opportunity to overtake, then re-run the system of motorcycle control to guide you while overtaking.

Information

Identify:

- a safe stretch of road along which you have adequate vision
- a gap into which you can safely return
- the speed of any approaching vehicles
- the relative speed of your own machine and the vehicle(s) you intend to overtake
- what is happening behind – consider the need for rear observation
- any road or landscape features that could conceal a rapidly approaching vehicle.

Consider the need to give information: is the driver in front aware of your presence, do you need to signal your intentions to the driver behind? Consider the benefits of giving a headlight, horn or indicator signal.

Position

Having made a thorough information check ahead and decided it is safe to go, consider the need for rear observation, give any necessary signals, and move out to an offside position. Generally, do this without accelerating. From this new position make a thorough information check of the road ahead and behind for any unidentified hazards. Decide whether to continue with overtaking.

Speed

Overtake if the situation is clear, adjusting your speed if necessary. While you are in the offside position you are in a zone of potential danger so move through it as briskly as possible.

Gear

Before overtaking you should have selected a suitable gear. Sometimes circumstances may require another gear change, but you should generally avoid this during the overtaking manoeuvre.

Acceleration

Adjust your speed to complete the overtaking manoeuvre safely, and to enter the gap you have identified. Where possible, use acceleration sense to adjust your speed, but use the brakes if necessary.

See Chapter 4, Acceleration, using gears and braking.

If you are overtaking in a line of traffic and the offside position provides a good view, consider the opportunity for further overtaking before you return to the nearside position. If you have considered all aspects of the system and it is safe to proceed, take the opportunity and move on to the new safe gap that you have identified.

Summary

The diagram below summarises the overtaking manoeuvre described in stage three:

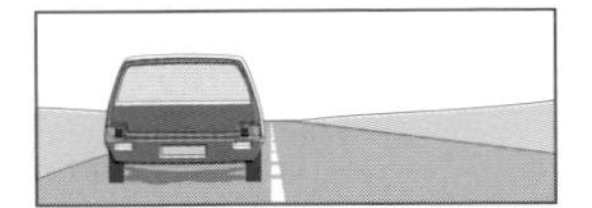

Position yourself to obtain the best view. If in doubt, hold back.

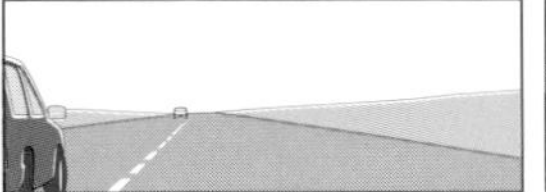

Overtake.

Move back to the near side in plenty of time.

Remember to consider rear observation before altering position or speed.

Practise the three-stage method of overtaking

Plan a route where there are likely to be hazards that will prevent you from overtaking immediately. Practise the three-stage overtaking method and then review your performance. Ask yourself the following questions:

- Did I have enough information to be sure I was safe at every stage?
- Was my positioning correct at every stage?
- Was I in the right gear at every stage?
- Did I always reach the return gap in good time?
- Was the return gap always big enough?
- Did I need to brake to return to the nearside?
- Did I miss any overtaking opportunities?

If you had any problems in these areas, work out why. Then work out how to overcome them in future.

Special hazards to consider before attempting to overtake

In the first part of this chapter we have worked through two methods for overtaking systematically. To present these as clearly as possible we have not introduced other aspects of road and traffic conditions which must be considered before overtaking. These considerations are essential to safety, and are explored next.

The *Highway Code* has a section which gives advice on overtaking. The illustrations below show some common accident situations that can arise if this advice is not followed.

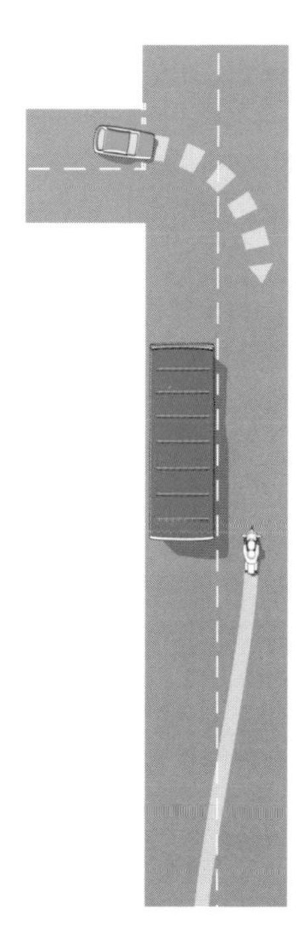

The rider does not realise that the driver of the blue car can see only the slow-moving bus and may move out into the path of the rider. This is a common cause of accidents when filtering.

The rider fails to foresee that the red car may turn without warning into a side road, cutting across the rider's path.

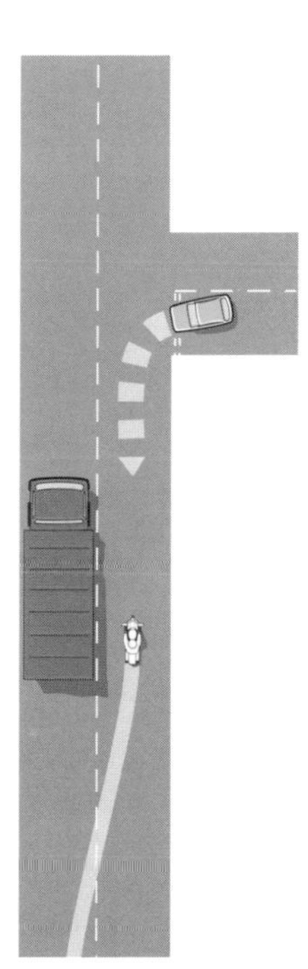

The rider fails to appreciate that the driver of the green car is looking only to his right and may pull out as the rider approaches on the wrong side of the road.

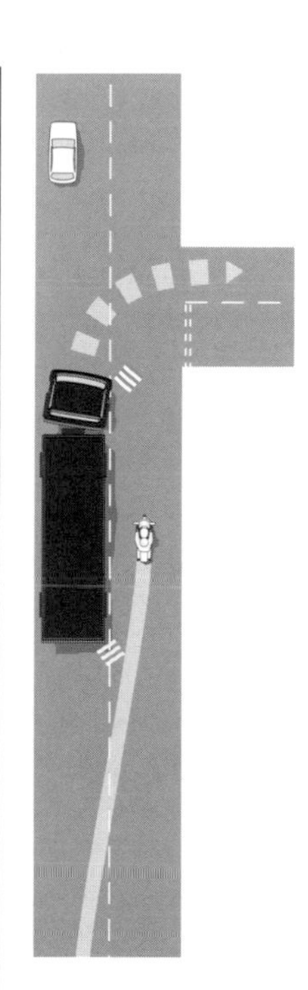

The rider fails to appreciate that the lorry is not indicating to overtake the car ahead, but is turning right.

The range of hazards you must consider

Before overtaking you must consider the full range of possible hazards that each situation presents:

- the vehicle in front
- the vehicles behind
- the road layout and conditions
- road surface
- overtaking in a stream of vehicles
- filtering
- overtaking on a single carriageway
- right-hand bends
- left-hand bends.
- overtaking on a dual carriageway

Each of these is discussed below.

The vehicle in front

Assess what sort of hazard the vehicle in front presents.

- Has the driver of the vehicle noticed you?
- Can you predict from earlier behaviour whether the response of the driver is likely to be aggressive?
- Does the size or the load of the vehicle prevent the driver from seeing you or prevent you from seeing the road ahead clearly?

Make your intention to overtake clear to the driver in front. Your road position and following distance help you to do this, but take care not to appear too intimidating. This can be counter-productive and provoke an aggressive response in the other driver who might speed up as you try to overtake. If the driver in front appears to be obstructive, consider the implications. Firstly, is it worthwhile overtaking at all and secondly, how much extra speed and space do you need to allow for this?

If the driver in front has not noticed your presence or has loads which obscure the rear view mirrors, take this into account. Be aware that if you cannot see the wing mirrors of an HGV, the driver cannot see you. Consider the use of the headlight or horn to inform the driver of your presence.

Take extra care before overtaking a long vehicle. If appropriate, take views to both sides of the vehicle and ensure that there is ample space to overtake and return safely to your own side. The same applies to vehicles that have wide or high loads: be sure that you have observed carefully and are aware of any possible dangers in the road ahead.

See Chapter 3, ***Observation,*** *page 52,* ***Anticipating the effects of wind.***

The vehicles behind

Assess whether the vehicles behind pose a risk. Note their speed, position and progress, and judge whether they may attempt to overtake you. Be aware that other vehicles may come forward from behind the vehicle behind you. Consider the need to signal your intentions. Use your mirrors and check to the side to monitor the situation behind you, especially before changing your speed or position. At higher speeds do not turn your head fully to look behind because the situation ahead may alter while your head is turned.

Road layout and conditions

When planning to overtake, consider the layout of the road ahead very carefully. Look for nearside obstructions or junctions (including pathways, tracks, entrances, farm gates) out of which vehicles or other hazards could emerge, and cause the vehicle(s) you intend to overtake suddenly to veer to the offside. On the offside, look carefully for junctions, especially where they could conceal emerging vehicles or other hazards.

Look for lay-bys on both sides of the road and be alert to the possibility that a vehicle might pull out of them. Be especially attentive to offside lay-bys. Drivers leaving them may not see you because they are concentrating on what is happening behind rather than in front of them. Try to position yourself so that drivers in nearside lay-bys can see you.

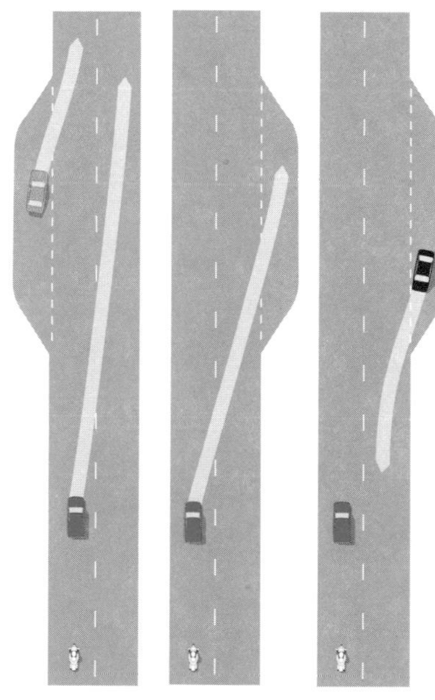

In each of these situations approaching lay-bys, the rider should be wary of overtaking. The arrows show the possible actions of traffic ahead.

Bends, hill crests, hump-back bridges and any other aspect of road layout which could obscure your view must be taken into account. Allow for the possibility that there are fast-moving vehicles approaching you on the sections of road you cannot see. Follow the basic rule for overtaking.

- **Identify a gap into which you can return and the point along the road at which you will be able to enter it.**
- **Judge whether you will be able to reach that point before any approaching vehicle, seen or unseen, could come into conflict with you. Coming into conflict includes causing either driver to alter course or speed or to be concerned for their safety. It does not refer only to the need to take drastic evasive action.**

You should have observed the whole stretch of road necessary to complete the manoeuvre, and know that it does not include any other hazards. Look especially for hazards which might cause the vehicles you are overtaking to alter their position. Make full use of road signs and road markings, especially those giving instructions or warning you of hazards ahead.

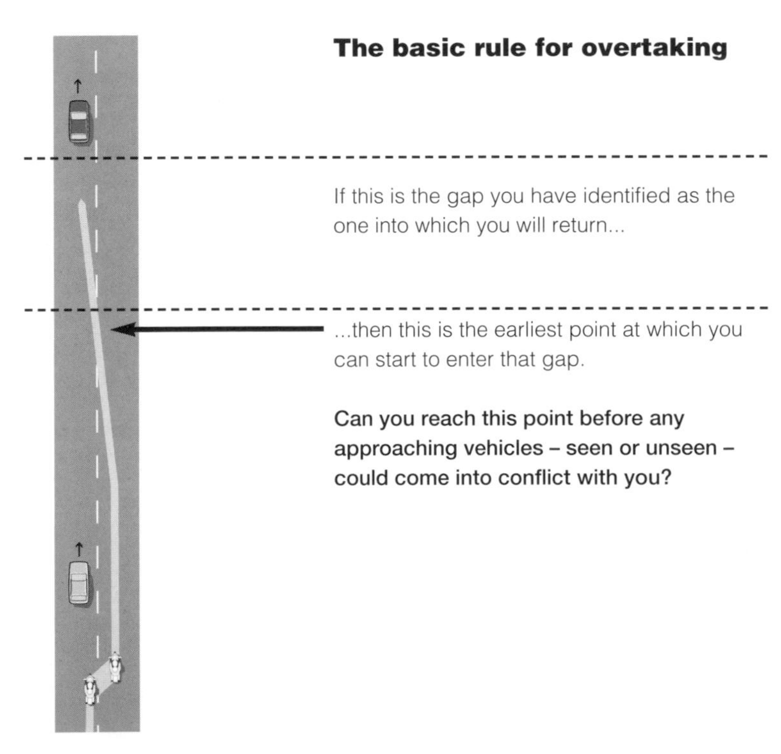

Road surface

The condition of the road surface should always be taken into account before you overtake. There may be ruts or holes which could throw a bike off course, deposits of diesel or other debris, which could require a change in course, or surface water which could cause a curtain of spray at a critical moment. The effects of adverse weather on road holding and visibility must always be taken into account.

See Chapter 3 Observation.

Overtaking in a stream of vehicles

Overtaking in a stream of vehicles is more difficult than overtaking an isolated vehicle because many more factors need to be considered. You have to take into account the possible actions of more drivers both in front and behind. There is always the possibility that drivers in front are not aware of your presence or intention to overtake and that drivers behind might attempt to overtake you.

Before overtaking, you should identify a clear gap between the vehicles in front which you can enter safely. Be aware that the gap may close up before you arrive, so choose gaps that are large enough to allow for this. Do not overtake if you will have to force your bike into a gap.

When overtaking in a stream of vehicles, consider positioning your machine on the offside section of the road. An offside position can improve your viewpoint because it is not obstructed by the vehicles in front, but this depends on the road layout. You can gain by holding this position if you can see that the road ahead is clear, and if you can identify a clear return gap and have sufficient time in which to reach it. When you reach the first return gap you may not need to enter it. If it is safe, hold the offside position to assess the possibility for further overtaking. Regard each vehicle as a separate hazard.

When you overtake clusters of vehicles, you must take extra care to ensure that the other drivers are aware of your presence.

Filtering

When traffic is stationary or moving slowly in queues, motorcyclists can use their manoeuvrability and limited space requirements to make progress. The advantages of filtering along or between stopped or slow moving traffic have to be weighed against the disadvantages of increased vulnerability while filtering.

If you decide to filter:

- take extreme care
- keep your speed low – you need to be able to stop suddenly if circumstances change
- always identify a place where you can rejoin the traffic flow before you move out
- make yourself visible – consider using dipped headlight
- be ready to brake and/or use the horn
- use the opportunity to make progress but be courteous and avoid conflict with other road users.

Watch out for and anticipate:

- pedestrians crossing between vehicles
- vehicles emerging from junctions
- vehicles changing lanes or U-turning without warning
- doors opening
- reflective paint and studs which could throw the bike off line
- traffic islands
- other bikes also filtering.

Overtaking on a single carriageway

Overtaking on a single carriageway is perhaps the most hazardous form of overtaking. While you are overtaking, your machine is in the path of any oncoming vehicles so great care must be taken before deciding on the manoeuvre.

Develop the ability to judge the speed and distance of oncoming vehicles accurately. You need to be able to assess whether you can reach the return gap before they do. Remember you always have the option of deciding not to overtake. Judging the speed of an oncoming vehicle is extremely difficult, especially on long straight roads. The size and type of the approaching vehicle may give you an indication of its possible speed.

Plan and prepare your overtaking carefully. As well as looking for vehicles, train yourself to look specifically for other motorcyclists, cyclists and pedestrians before you overtake. If you do not expect to see something, you may not see it when it is there – an oncoming pedestrian or cyclist can be easily overlooked.

Overtaking on bends

Right-hand bends

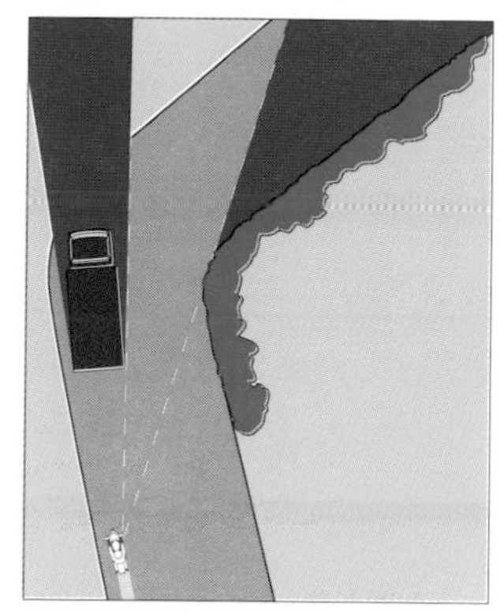

Where the vehicle in front is approaching the apex of a right-hand bend with a restricted view, consider a position to the nearside provided the road surface is good.

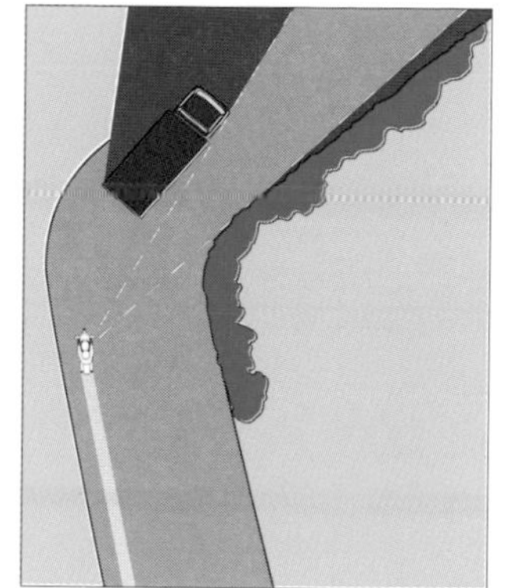

Move up on the vehicle in front just before it reaches the apex so that you gain the earliest possible view along its offside.

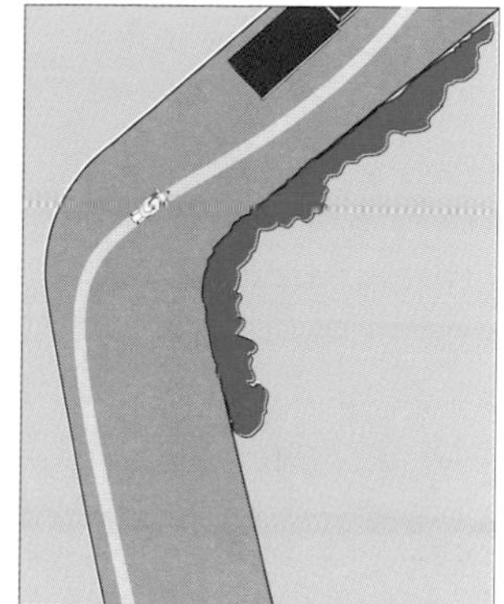

Overtake if the road is clear, as long as there is no risk of losing tyre adhesion and you have adequate nearside clearance during the manoeuvre. If conditions are not favourable for overtaking, drop back.

Left-hand bends

Where the leading vehicle approaches a blind left bend do not attempt to overtake until you have a clear view of the road ahead.

You could maintain a position where you can see along the nearside of the leading vehicle as it passes through the bend.

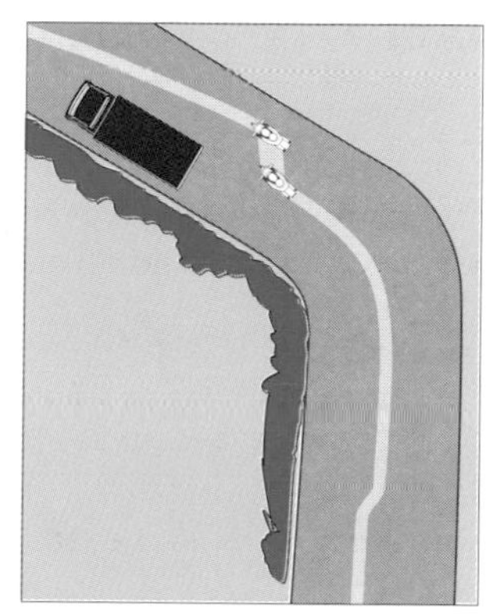

If this view is favourable move out to look along the offside as the road straightens and start to overtake when conditions are suitable. Bear in mind that areas of the road will be obscured while you change from a nearside to an offside view, so take great care when you do this.

obstructed vision

Single carriageway roads marked with three lanes

Single carriageway roads marked with three lanes are inherently dangerous as the overtaking lane in each direction is the shared centre lane. Never attempt to overtake if there is the possibility of an approaching vehicle moving into the centre lane. Avoid overtaking when you would make a third line of moving vehicles unless you are sure it is absolutely safe to do so.

Avoid the temptation to follow another vehicle through an apparently safe gap on a three-lane single carriageway. Always assess a safe return position for yourself. The leading vehicle may well be able to slip safely into place on the nearside leaving you stranded in the middle facing oncoming vehicles. When travelling in a group of bikes avoid the temptation to 'follow my leader' when overtaking. Always fully assess the safety of each overtaking manoeuvre for yourself.

When you are judging speed and distance to overtake and a vehicle is approaching, look out for the presence of the 'lurker'. This is a vehicle which closes right up behind other vehicles and then sweeps out into full view. Do not assume that the drivers of light vehicles or cars behind a heavy lorry are content to stay where they are. They could well pull out just when you are overtaking. The lurker can occur on any road and is just as dangerous on a long straight level piece of two-way road. If you suspect a lurker, move to the nearside to reduce the danger and increase your visibility. Do not move over so far as to encourage an approaching lurker to attempt to overtake.

Overtaking on dual carriageways

On dual carriageways it can be more difficult to judge the speed of traffic approaching from the rear.

See Chapter 9, ***Motorway riding*** *and the* **Highway Code**.

Before overtaking carefully observe the vehicles in the nearside lanes. If one of them is closing up on the vehicle in front, the driver may pull out, possibly without signalling or only signalling as the vehicle starts to move out. A good guide is the distance between the wheels of the vehicle and the lane markings. If the gap narrows it could be moving out.

If possible, avoid overtaking when it would result in three vehicles being abreast, although on many motorways, because of the volume of traffic, it can be difficult to avoid this situation. Always overtake on the right on dual carriageways, except when traffic is moving in queues and the queue on the right is moving more slowly than you are.

See Chapter 3, *Observation*, page 52, *Anticipating the effects of wind.*

Remember when you overtake a large vehicle that you may be buffeted by the slip stream. In high winds you may suddenly encounter strong cross-winds as you move beyond the shelter of a large vehicle. In both situations take a firmer hold on the handlebars as you pass, but keep your arms and body flexible so as not to unbalance the machine.

Practise observation skills for overtaking

Over the next two weeks make a note of any overtaking situations that you misjudge. Add to this list any dangerous or potentially dangerous misjudgements you can remember making in the past. For each situation work out the observational errors that caused you to misjudge the situation.

Ask yourself if any errors occur consistently. Do you make specific errors such as failing to take account of obscured junctions, or is the problem a general lack of observation? Plan how to improve your observation so that you can avoid making the same mistakes in the future.

Assisting others to overtake

Assisting others to overtake eases tensions and improves the quality of driving for everyone on the road. The key element is your attitude of mind when you ride. You should not regard riding as a competition but as a means of travelling between two points as safely as possible. Try to regard your riding dispassionately and keep an eye on yourself to identify any inappropriate responses. If other road users wish to overtake you, assist them:

- be alert to the intentions of riders and drivers behind you: use your mirrors and assess whether they wish to overtake or not
- allow enough distance between you and the vehicle in front for the overtaking vehicle to enter the gap.

Be aware that other motorists do not keep to speed limits. This is likely to happen:

- when you slow down to enter a lower speed limit area
- when you are about to leave a lower speed limit area.

Review

In this chapter we have looked at:

- how to overtake safely
- how to overtake in the absence of other hazards
- the three-stage approach to overtaking when other hazards cause you to take up a following position
- the hazards that you should consider before overtaking.

Check your understanding

What makes overtaking potentially hazardous?

What are the eight safety points that you should follow for overtaking?

If you are in doubt about overtaking what should you do?

What are the hazards that would make it necessary to follow another vehicle before overtaking?

What is the three-stage approach to overtaking and when is it used?

When you move out before overtaking, what should you check?

What do you need to consider about the driver in front before overtaking?

What do you need to consider about road layout and conditions before overtaking?

What hazards should you look for when filtering?

When can it be useful to hold an offside position?

How can you help others to overtake?

If you have difficulty in answering any of these questions, look back over the relevant part of this chapter to refresh your memory.

Use this chapter to find out:

- what to do before you join the motorway
- how to join the motorway
- what to do on the motorway, including lane discipline
- how to leave the motorway
- how to deal with specific hazards on the motorway.

Chapter 9

Motorway riding

Developing your skill at motorway riding

Safe motorway riding depends on the careful application of the skills and methods of riding that you have learnt in the other chapters of *Motorcycle Roadcraft*, together with an awareness of the extra hazards that arise from the speed and volume of the traffic. This chapter identifies those hazards and ways of dealing with them. You do not need to develop special techniques for dealing with motorways, but you do have to apply the techniques you have learnt all the more rigorously because of the testing conditions.

Although this chapter is called motorway riding, much of it is applicable to riding on dual carriageways. The speed limit for motorcycles is the same on many dual carriageways as it is on motorways, but the absence of a hard shoulder and the presence of lay-bys and crossroads make dual carriageways especially hazardous.

Before you join the motorway

The *Highway Code*

The *Highway Code* contains advice on motorway riding, and includes information on motorway signs and regulations. You should know these sections thoroughly. This chapter discusses the techniques which will help you to implement the *Highway Code* advice more effectively.

Special features of motorways

You need to prepare adequately before you join a motorway.

These are the special conditions you should consider:

- the speed and volume of the traffic
- the limited occurrence of rest and refuelling areas
- the dangers of stopping on the hard shoulder
- the level of attention required
- the legal limitations on certain vehicles using the motorway.

Each of these affects your safety. High speeds mean that hazardous situations develop quickly and that you travel further before you can react. Minimum stopping distances are greatly extended and collisions often cause death, serious injury and damage. As the volume of traffic increases, the demands on your attention and decision-making also increase. With more vehicles there are more hazards and the opportunities for manoeuvre are more restricted.

You need to maintain a high level of concentration, which is difficult in monotonous conditions. Fatigue is a real problem and you should always plan adequate rest breaks. The limited opportunities for stopping on motorways require riders to be in good health and their machines in good condition. The risk of collision makes stopping on the hard shoulder extremely hazardous for the rider and for other motorway users.

We shall now look at the safety implications of these special features of motorways for:

- the rider
- the motorcycle
- traffic, road and surface conditions.

The rider

The high speeds of motorway traffic cause dangerous situations to develop very rapidly. Experience is required to cope with your own speed and the speed of other vehicles. It takes time to develop skills in accurately assessing high speeds and stopping distances at these speeds. Always ride well within your own competence and aim to steadily develop your experience so that you are fully comfortable within your existing speed range before moving on to higher speeds.

Fatigue

See Chapter 1, *Becoming a better rider*.

Fatigue is the cause of a disproportionate number of accidents on motorways. As you tire, your ability to take in and process information is reduced and your ability to react to the information you have received takes longer. Fatigue is most likely in conditions which are relatively unchanging – for example, riding for long periods in lower density traffic, or in fog or at night. If you get wet or cold you are at increased risk of fatigue. Wear waterproofs before going on a motorway if rain is expected and wear clothes that provide sufficient warmth. You should know how to cope with fatigue. This is fully discussed in Chapter 1 so look back and refresh your memory if necessary.

Health, medication and emotional state

See Chapter 1, *Becoming a better rider*, page 19, *Health, medication and emotional state*.

Do not ride on a motorway if you are feeling unwell or are taking medication that impairs your judgement. Also be aware that emotional distress can impair your judgement.

Route plan

Plan your route and know where your rest, refuelling and exit points are before you undertake a motorway journey. Do not be tempted to look at maps or route planners fixed to your petrol tank or tank bag while moving. Consulting maps while riding is dangerous, and must not be done on motorways or any other road.

The motorcycle

Remember to carry out a roadworthiness check before you start your journey.

Before you start a journey that will take you on to a motorway, run through a

See *Roadworthiness check*, page 172.

P petrol **O** oil **W** water **E** electrics **R** rubber (tyres)

check.

Traffic, road and surface conditions

Consider the likely traffic volume and the possibility of roadworks and other delays. These affect how long your journey will take, and allowances should be made for them so that you are not rushing to meet deadlines. As delays mount up it may be worth considering another route or cancelling your journey altogether. Where weather conditions are deteriorating you should consider very carefully whether to make your journey at all. In foggy conditions it is essential that you are familiar with the *Highway Code* fog code and use it. Further advice on fog is given below and in Chapter 3, 'Observation'. During and after rain, heavy spray from large vehicles travelling fast restricts visibility. Consider using a dipped headlight and, if safe to do so, overtake in the lane furthest away.Your safety depends on adapting your riding to the prevailing road and weather conditions – this is crucial on motorways.

Joining the motorway

Which lane is which?

This chapter uses the numbering system used by the police and other emergency services to refer to motorway lanes.

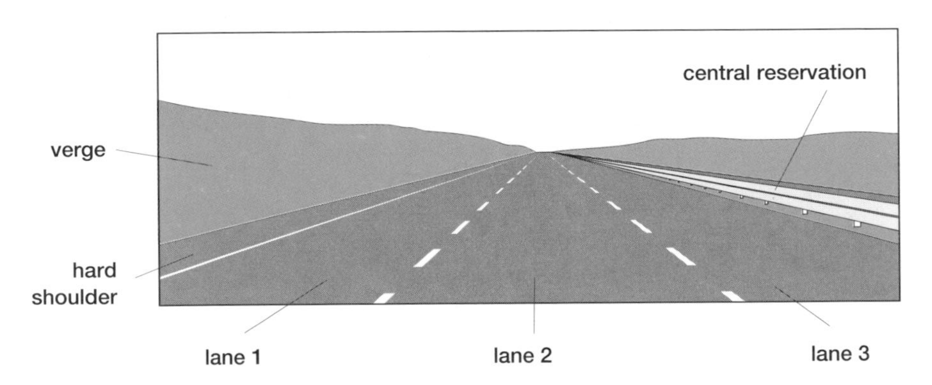

The nearside lane is lane 1, and the other lanes are numbered in sequence to the furthest offside lane. On a three-lane motorway lane 1 is the lane next to the hard shoulder and lane 3 is the lane next to the central reservation. The hard shoulder is not counted as a carriageway lane.

Joining the motorway at a slip road or where motorways merge is hazardous and you should use the system of motorcycle control to approach and join. Slip roads are designed to give riders the time and space to merge smoothly with traffic on the main carriageway. They are often elevated and you should take advantage of the high viewpoint to observe the traffic flow and to plan your approach. Skilful use of the system should enable you to join the motorway without causing other drivers to alter course or speed. Remember the value of rear observation to check the traffic on the motorway before selecting a gap in the nearest lane. Drivers on the motorway have priority and may not be able to move over to allow you to enter, but with early vision, planning and acceleration sense you should be able to merge safely. Only poor planning or exceptionally heavy traffic will cause you to stop in the acceleration lane.

Slip roads have one or more lanes. If you are travelling in an offside lane of the slip road, consider how your speed and position will affect the access of nearside vehicles on to the motorway. If you overtake a vehicle to your nearside just before joining the motorway you could block its path. You are in danger of colliding with it if you cannot move straight into lane 2 of the motorway.

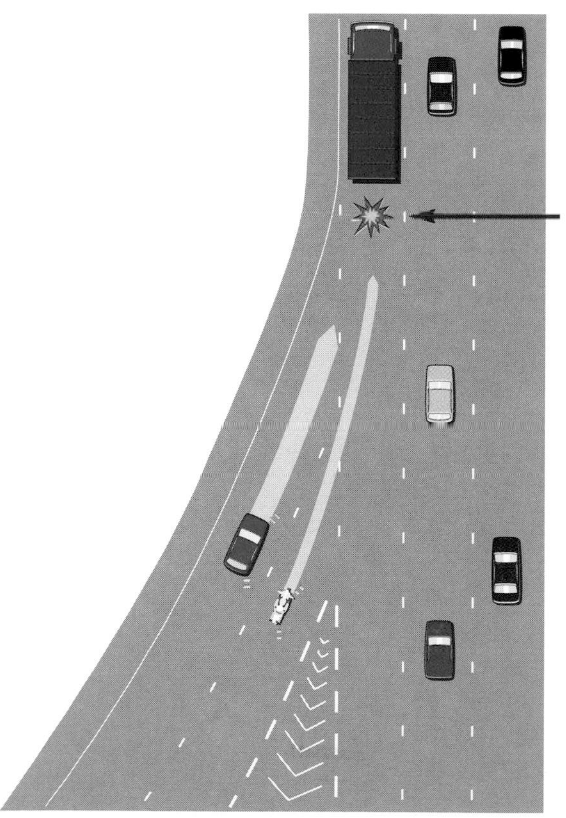

Do not overtake a vehicle travelling in the inside lane of the slip road if this would block the entry of that vehicle on to the motorway.

Use the system

As you enter the motorway all five phases of the system are relevant. You need to take sufficient **information** about the traffic on the slip road and motorway to ensure that you are in the right **position**, at the right **speed**, and in the right **gear** to **accelerate** on to the motorway smoothly and in safety.

Signalling

Before entering lane 1 of the motorway consider giving a signal to inform motorists already on the motorway of your intention to join the traffic flow.

Before you join the motorway, quickly check over your shoulder to make sure there is nothing in your blind spot. Good use of your mirrors on the approach will allow you to reduce the time spent doing this to a minimum.

Acceleration

As the speeds on motorways are higher than on the rest of the road system, you should allow yourself time to adjust to riding at speed and to the speeds of other vehicles.

Observation

Because of the speeds involved, extended observation on the motorway is essential:

- look ahead and behind you right up to the road horizons
- scan ahead, to the sides and to the rear frequently and thoroughly
- use your mirrors regularly – you should know at all times what is happening behind you
- be aware of the blind spots to the side and behind your machine and those of other drivers
- monitor what is happening to your machine – regularly check that the instruments are giving normal readings, listen to the sound of your engine and to the noise of the tyres on the road surface
- check your speed regularly on the speedometer – it is very easy to increase speed without realising it
- be especially alert around junctions – traffic patterns change rapidly in these areas.

Adapting to higher speeds

At 70 miles per hour you travel 31 metres per second (over 100 ft per second). At such speeds you need as much time to react as possible:

See Chapter 3, ***Observation****, page 44,* ***Use your eyes - scanning*** *and Chapter 4,* ***Acceleration, using gears and braking****, page 80,* ***The safe stopping distance rule****.*

- extend your observations in all directions and to the road horizons to give yourself more time
- anticipate early and maintain a safe following distance – in good weather the two-second rule provides a good guide but in poor weather conditions this distance needs to be greatly extended
- avoid coarse manoeuvres at speed
- give other drivers sufficient time to see and react to your signals before making a manoeuvre
- wind and engine noise can drown the sound of your horn at high speeds, so consider using your headlight as an alternative.

On your next three motorway journeys, practise extending your observation. Make a point of scanning as far as the road horizon, front and back. Use rear observation frequently. Regularly scan to the sides as well.

Your aim is to equip yourself with the longest possible time in which to react. Active scanning helps you to maintain a generally high level of attention, which increases your overall safety.

Lane discipline

Good lane discipline is essential for motorway riding. There are no slow or fast lanes. Overtake only to the right, except when traffic is moving slowly in queues and the queue on your right is moving more slowly than you are. Always consider rear observation before changing lanes in either direction.

Do not move to a lane on your left to overtake.

Overtaking

Before overtaking be alert for:

- slower vehicles moving out in front of you
- faster vehicles coming up behind you.

Apply the system of motorcycle control to overtake safely on motorways and pay special attention to the information phase.

Taking information

The high speeds of motorway traffic make it necessary to take information carefully before making any manoeuvre. Scan regularly so that you are continually aware of the pattern of surrounding traffic. You should know which vehicles are closing up on other vehicles in front, and which vehicles are moving up behind. Constantly monitor opportunities to overtake and match your speed of approach to coincide with an opportunity. Make allowances for the additional hazards presented by lane closures and motorway junctions.

Look for early warnings of the intention of other road users to overtake. Indications of another driver's intention to move out are:

- relative speeds
- head movements
- body movements
- vehicle movement from the centre of the lane towards the white lane markers.

You are likely to see all these before the driver signals: many drivers, if they signal at all, only signal as they start to change lanes.

> Over a motorway journey of reasonable length (say 20 miles), practise watching for the indications above and try to predict, before they start indicating, when other drivers are about to change lanes.
>
> Use this anticipation to help your planning.

Overtaking on left-hand bends when lanes 1 and 2 are mainly occupied by heavy goods or large vehicles needs to be considered carefully. There is always the possibility that a car is hidden between the heavy goods vehicles and is about to pull out into lane 3. Do not attempt to overtake unless you are sure you can see all the vehicles in lane 2 and well into the gaps between them so you can be sure no small vehicles are concealed.

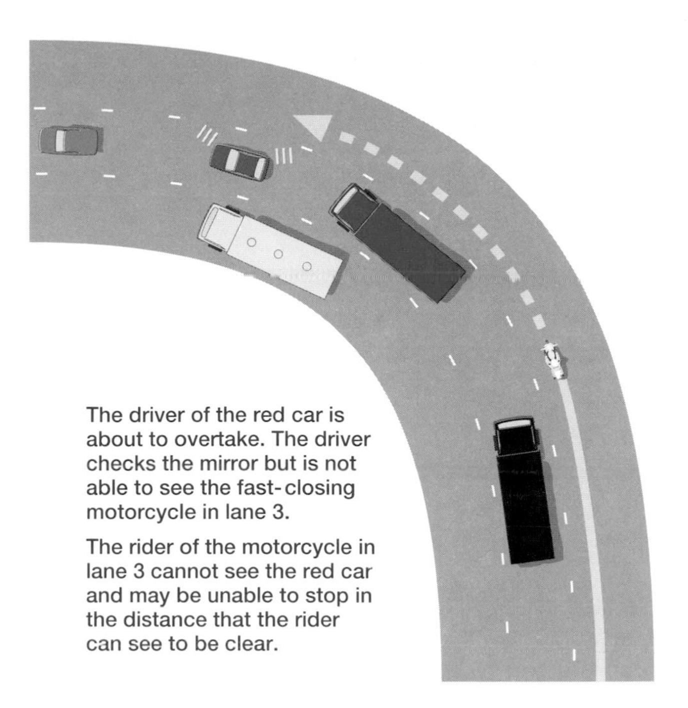

The driver of the red car is about to overtake. The driver checks the mirror but is not able to see the fast-closing motorcycle in lane 3.

The rider of the motorcycle in lane 3 cannot see the red car and may be unable to stop in the distance that the rider can see to be clear.

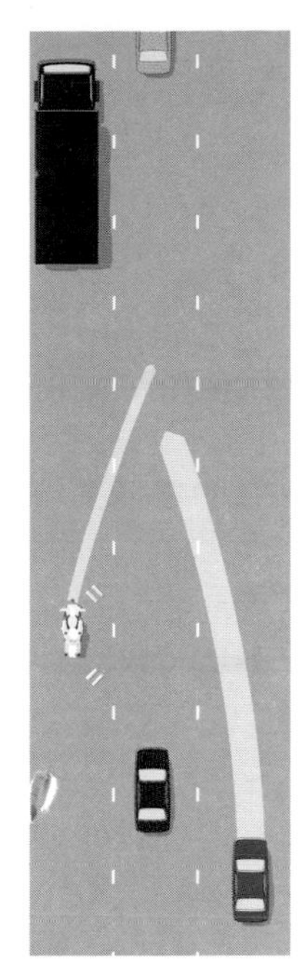

As you move from lane 1 to lane 2, beware of vehicles moving up behind you into lane 2 from lane 3.

Just before you overtake make a thorough check of the position and speed of the vehicles behind. Move your head to reduce the extent of any blind spots. Recheck the position and speed of vehicles to the front and then consider the information that you need to give to the surrounding traffic.

Giving information

Consider alerting other drivers to your presence especially if you are travelling at speed. If you decide a headlight signal would be helpful, give it in sufficient time for the other driver to react. The purpose of a headlight warning is to inform other drivers of your presence. Give a single flash, extending its length according to your speed and the response of other drivers. Take care not to appear aggressive to other drivers, and be aware of the possibility of dazzling oncoming drivers. Also be careful that your headlight flash is not misinterpreted as an invitation to other drivers to move out in front of you.

Indicator signals

Consider giving an indicator signal before changing lanes. Let the indicator flash long enough for other drivers to see and react to it.

When you have passed the vehicle or vehicles in front, return to lane 1 when a suitable opportunity arises but avoid excessive weaving.

Overtaking situations to avoid

You should generally avoid overtaking when to do so would create a line of three vehicles travelling abreast. In current traffic conditions this is often not possible but you should avoid situations like the one illustrated below which leave you no room for manoeuvre.

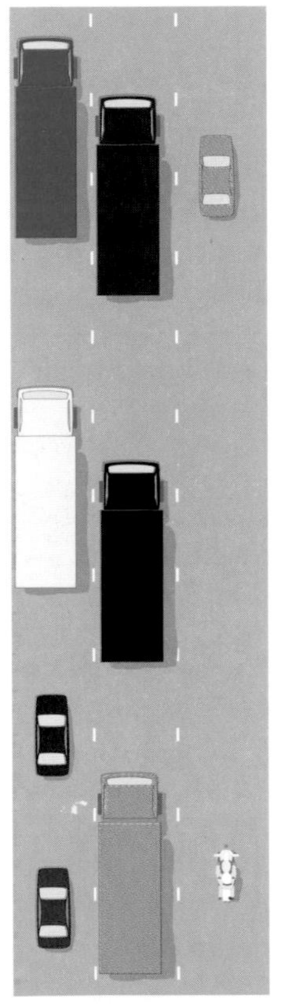

This illustrates a problem for vehicles moving at speed and overtaking three abreast. The overtaking rider has no room for manoeuvre if a hazard arises. Movement into lane 1 or 2 is blocked by the vehicles in those lanes and escape through lane 3 is blocked by the vehicle ahead.

Wind turbulence from the large vehicles may severely destabilise your machine. Hold back until the vehicle in lane 3 has moved ahead of the vehicles in lane 2. This gives you the option of an alternative position. Keep a watchful eye on your mirrors for vehicles closing up fast behind you.

Being overtaken

Anticipate the movement of vehicles behind you by their lane position and their speed of approach. By observing minor details in the way the traffic is behaving you will be forewarned before any signals or manoeuvres are made. This will help you to avoid potentially dangerous situations. Be aware that, as you are overtaken, you temporarily enter a blind spot for the overtaking driver.

Motorway junctions

At junctions and service areas, there are likely to be variations in the speed of the traffic flow and an increase in the number of vehicles changing lanes. Watch for drivers who delay changing lanes for an exit to the last second. When you see a motorway exit, anticipate the possibility of an entry slip road ahead and traffic joining the motorway.

If you are on the main carriageway, check your mirrors early and if possible allow traffic to join the motorway by making slight adjustments to your speed or changing to a lane on your right. However, do not move to a lane on your right if it forces existing motorway users to change their speed or position. Ultimately it is the vehicle joining the motorway that should give way, but be prepared in case it does not.

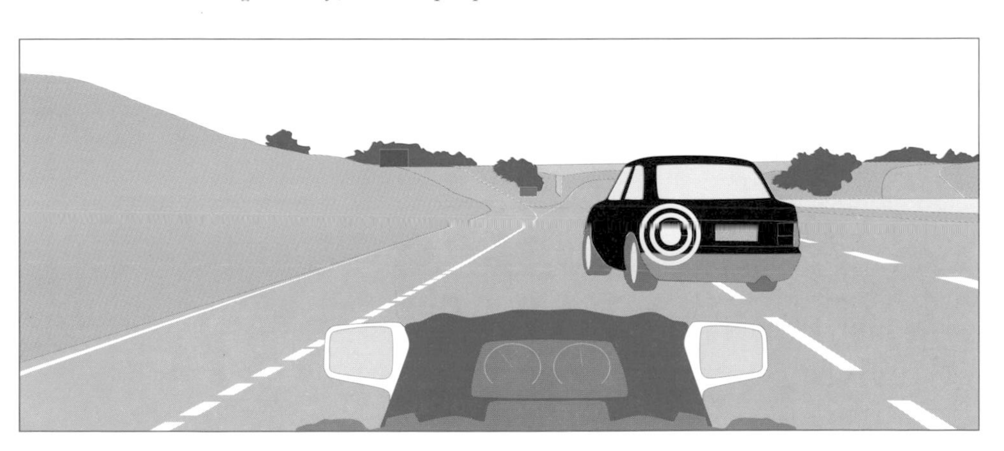

Watch for drivers who delay changing lanes for an exit road to the last second, and watch for traffic joining the motorway by slip roads ahead.

Leaving the motorway

Leaving the motorway should be carefully planned. Know well in advance at which junction you intend to leave. Assess the road and traffic conditions as you approach it and make use of the information provided by road signs and markings.

Exit information

The diagram below illustrates the exit information given at most motorway exits.

One mile from the exit a direction sign gives the junction number and the roads leading off the exit

At a half mile from the exit the same information is repeated on the direction sign plus the town or destination names

At 300 yards from the exit deceleration lane there is a marker post

Further marker posts are positioned at the 200 yard and 100 yard points before the start of the deceleration lane

A third large sign at the beginning of the deceleration lane also adds principal destinations ahead

As you approach your intended exit junction look for the advance direction boards and use the system of motorcycle control to plan and carry out your exit. If the motorway is busy, consider joining the left-hand lane earlier rather than later. Always allow sufficient time for other drivers to react to your signals. Generally you should indicate no later than the 300 yard marker and if it would benefit other drivers you should indicate well before. If your machine has self-cancelling indicators, monitor them to make sure they do not switch off too soon.

Avoid braking on the main carriageway and plan to lose any unwanted road speed in the deceleration lane. On busy motorways be alert for vehicles attempting to leave the motorway late from the second or third lane and cutting across your path. Remember that high speeds will affect your perception of speed when you leave the motorway:

- check your speedometer regularly to help you adjust to the lower speeds of the ordinary road system
- plan for the point at which you will meet two-way traffic
- be alert for acute bends at the end of exit slip roads and watch for road paint, oil and tyre dust deposits which make these areas exceptionally slippery.

A route direction sign is usually placed at the point where the deceleration lane separates from the main carriageway

Over the next month pay attention to the way you use the system of motorcycle control to leave a motorway. Include planned exits from the motorway from positions starting in lane 1, lane 2 and lane 3. Pay particular attention to the information phase. After you have completed an exit, assess whether it went according to your riding plan, and whether you considered all the relevant phases of the system. If not, work out how you could improve the manoeuvre next time.

Special hazards

There are a number of special hazards which you need to take account of on motorway journeys. At high speeds the destabilising effects of large vehicle slip streams increases and overall safe stopping distances greatly increase. Safe riding depends on the basic rule: always ride so that you are able to stop in the distance you can see to be clear. This will vary with the density of traffic, weather conditions and the other hazards described in this section. If this advice were systematically followed, motorway pile-ups would not occur.

Weather conditions

*For further advice about dealing with the weather conditions described in this section, see Chapter 3, **Observation**, page 50, **Weather conditions**.*

Poor weather conditions can reduce visibility and road holding. At high speed the effects of these hazards are increased. When visibility is restricted you should reduce speed and consider using your headlight and foglight. You must use them if visibility drops below 100 metres. A useful guide for assessing visibility is the gap between motorway marker posts which is approximately 100 metres. Bear in mind that the rear foglight can mask the brakelight and dazzle the driver behind. You must switch it off when visibility improves.

Fog

Fog is particularly dangerous on motorways. It reduces riders' perception of speed and their perception of risk because they cannot see; at the same time it encourages them to drive closer together in order to keep sight of the vehicle lights ahead. Be alert to the risks from the reckless behaviour of other drivers.

See also the fog code in the **Highway Code**.

In freezing fog at higher speeds, mist and spray can rapidly freeze on your visor and windscreen and further reduce visibility. Use anti-mist sprays and treatments to reduce this to a minimum.

To stop in the distance you can see to be clear in variable fog, you must adjust your speed to the actual density of the fog banks you are riding through, not to some imagined 'safe' speed for foggy conditions. If your road speed is low enough, which is likely in conditions of low visibility, consider raising your visor to improve your view. Riding in fog is extremely tiring, so watch for signs of fatigue and take more rest if necessary.

Rain

At speed the hazards from rain and water lying on the surface of the road increase. Heavy spray caused by tyres cutting through water can reduce visibility to a few feet, and you should allow for this, especially while overtaking. Water lying on the road surface can build up to form a wedge of water between the tyres and the road causing aquaplaning: this results in instant and complete loss of control.

See Chapter 5, ***Cornering, balance and avoiding skids****, page 105,* ***Aquaplaning*** *for further advice.*

After a long, hot, dry spell a deposit of tyre and other dust builds up on the road surface. These deposits create a slippery surface especially during and after rain. Take precautions to retain tyre grip in these conditions.

Snow and sleet

Snow and sleet reduce visibility and reduce tyre traction. At speed, spray thrown up by the wheels of the vehicle in front reduces visibility further, and stability problems arise when ruts develop in the snow. Often stability can only be maintained by travelling at walking pace with both feet ready to support the bike. In heavy snow consider whether your journey is really necessary.

Ice

Pay particular attention to your speed and following distances in potentially icy conditions, especially if the freezing conditions develop suddenly and the road surface is not gritted.

High winds

Motorways are often elevated above the surrounding countryside and tend to suffer from the effects of high winds. Be prepared for particularly strong gusts of wind on leaving cuttings, entering or emerging from under a bridge, crossing dales and going into open country. Take particular care on top of viaducts and bridges.

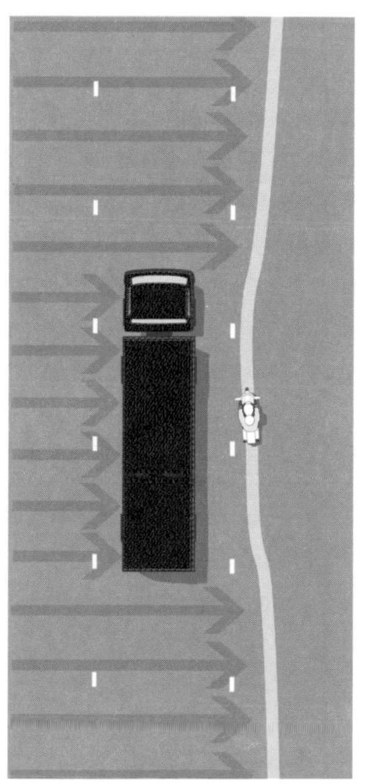

In windy conditions high-sided vehicles may suddenly veer; they also tend to act as wind breaks causing heavy buffeting to smaller vehicles as they draw past them. In these conditions, keep a firm grip on the handlebars with both hands.

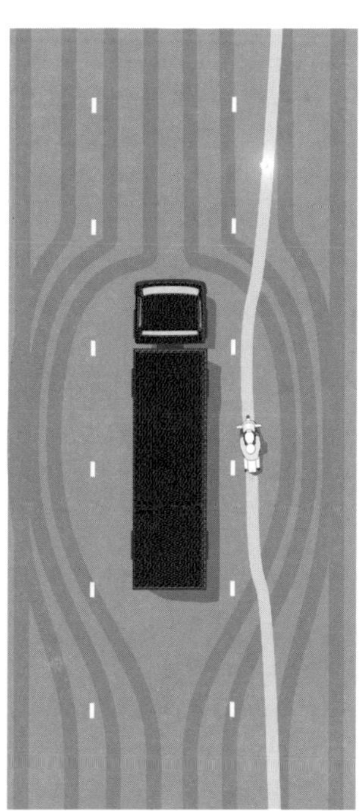

Wind effects are also caused by the slip stream of high-sided vehicles. This pulls smaller vehicles towards the larger vehicle during overtaking. As the smaller vehicle moves in front it breaks free of the suction and has a tendency to veer away. Counter this by a firm grip on the handlebars and consider leaning the machine into the wind to compensate the sideways force.

Bright sun

Bright sunshine in the hours just after sunrise and before sunset can cause serious dazzle, especially on east/west sections of road. When the sun is shining in your mirrors, adjust them to give you the best visibility with the minimum of glare. Be aware that drivers in front will have similar problems in seeing behind, and allow for this when overtaking.

Debris

Regularly scan the road surface for debris which may have fallen from vehicles and bridges. This can cause other vehicles to alter course suddenly and can damage tyres.

Lane closures

Roadworks are regularly encountered on motorway journeys. Contraflow systems are not dangerous in themselves but become dangerous when road users fail to respond to advance warnings. All roadworks are signed on approach and the sequence of the signs is always the same and should be known. You should conform to the mandatory speed limits that often accompany roadworks, even when conditions seem to be suitable for a higher speed.

Merging with other traffic requires judgement and courtesy. A sensible policy is for vehicles from each lane to merge alternately. These situations have great potential for unnecessary conflict and therefore unnecessary accidents. Allow adequate following gaps, and do not close up tightly to prevent other vehicles merging.

Matrix signs and signals are used on motorways to warn of speed restrictions, lane closures or other changes in riding conditions ahead. You may not immediately be able to see the need to slow down or change lanes. Do not be complacent and assume the sign is a mistake. The incident it refers to may be some distance along the motorway.

Matrix signs warn of hazards that may be some distance ahead.

General safety rules

Although there are fewer accidents per mile travelled on motorways than other roads, they can be extremely hazardous places. You should follow these general safety rules at all times:

- ensure you have sufficient fuel to reach the next service station
- maintain lane discipline at all times
- maintain a safe following distance at all times – avoid riding too close to the vehicle in front
- always be able to stop safely in the distance you can see to be clear
- make allowances for cross-winds and the turbulence caused by large vehicles
- do not walk on the carriageway
- do not turn to look at accidents on your own or the other carriageway but anticipate the likelihood of other drivers slowing down to look
- do not use or block emergency crossing points
- plan your route in advance – know your intended exit junction number
- be alert and take active steps to prevent boredom and fatigue
- concentrate fully and use your mirrors often
- give signals in plenty of time
- know the meanings of the different road signs, matrix and gantry signals used on motorways
- do not exceed your own or your machine's capabilities.

Review

In this chapter we have looked at:

- the special features of motorways
- why motorways can be hazardous
- what safety points you should always consider about the rider, the machine and road conditions before you use a motorway
- how to identify the lanes of a motorway
- how to join a motorway
- the importance of extended observation, especially when riding at speed
- how to overtake on a motorway
- the additional hazards at motorway junctions
- how to leave a motorway
- weather conditions and other special hazards
- what to do at lane closures
- general safety rules for riding on motorways.

Check your understanding

What are the special features of motorways that you need to consider before starting a journey?

Why should you not ride on a motorway if you are feeling tired or unwell?

Why can it be hazardous to overtake a vehicle on the acceleration lane just as you join a motorway?

At 70 mph how many metres do you travel in one second?

Apart from indicator lights, what are the possible early signs that another vehicle is going to change lanes?

What signals might you consider giving before overtaking?

What is the typical series of signs, starting from the 1 mile sign, that mark a motorway exit junction?

What lights should you have on when visibility is below 100 metres on the motorway?

What speed should you ride at in fog?

Describe at least three other hazards that can create particular problems on motorways, and explain how you would plan to deal with them.

If you have difficulty in answering any of these questions, look back over the relevant part of this chapter to refresh your memory.

Use this chapter to find out:

- the principles for assessing a safe speed
- other factors to take into account when assessing a safe speed.

Chapter 10

Speed and safety

Safety

The first part of this chapter looks at the effects of speed on safety and at the factors you must consider when assessing a safe speed: these include the capabilities of the rider and the machine, and the prevailing road, traffic and weather conditions. The second part of the chapter looks in detail at how speed affects the rider and at the key points that will help you to use speed safely.

Speed has a major impact on safety. International evidence clearly shows that lower speed limits result in fewer accidents. In Chapter 1 we saw that drivers who drive fast regardless of the circumstances have an accident risk three to five times greater than drivers who do not. At greater speeds the risks obviously increase – you approach hazards faster, you have less time to react, and the impact damage is greater. A child hit by a car at 20 mph may be injured but will probably live: a child hit at 40 mph will probably die.

Risks increase with speed but whatever your speed, if it is inappropriate in the circumstances, it is dangerous. This concept is central to the system of motorcycle control and you will have encountered the idea throughout *Motorcycle Roadcraft*. It is most clearly expressed in the safe stopping distance rule:

Ride so that you are able to stop safely on your own side of the road in the distance you can see to be clear.

This rule identifies the maximum speed at which it is safe to ride. It requires you to take account of all the circumstances before deciding the appropriate speed and to adjust your speed as circumstances alter. The capabilities of the rider and machine, and the prevailing road, traffic and weather conditions, must all be taken into account.

The rider

As we saw in Chapter 1 there are both internal and external pressures which will at times encourage you to ride faster than your competence or the circumstances justify. Skilful riders recognise these pressures and take steps to counter them.

Always ride within your competence, at a speed which is appropriate to the circumstances.

As you become more experienced your level of confidence may increase but this will not necessarily make you a safer rider. You will only be safe if you also develop appropriate attitudes, recognise your own vulnerability and accurately evaluate risks.

> Do you always ride within your competence? Can you recall situations when you were riding too fast for your own comfort? If so, why was it? Were any of the situations similar? How can you avoid repeating them in the future?

The machine

Different machines have different handling characteristics. When you ride an unfamiliar machine allow yourself time to get used to its controls and handling characteristics before riding fast. Allow an extra safety margin until you are confident about how the bike will respond. This is particularly important in respect of wobble and weave.

Wobble and weave

Wobble and weave describe two types of machine instability that develop in certain circumstances and can be extremely dangerous. The conditions in which they develop vary with the individual machine, so it is essential that you fully understand the characteristics of the individual machines you ride before riding them at speed.

- Wobble is of two types: medium speed wobble, which develops at speeds around 35 mph, and high speed wobble, which occurs at much higher speeds. In both cases the steering head and handlebars start to wobble. At high speeds the wobble becomes progressively more pronounced causing total loss of control.

  Control medium speed wobble by taking a firmer grip on the handlebars and altering the road speed to take it out of the unstable range.

  High speed wobble is very difficult to control.

- Weave occurs when the back wheel starts to oscillate from side to side. There are two types: high speed straight road weave and cornering weave.

  High speed straight road weave tends to increase with speed so you cannot accelerate through it. To regain control, lean forward to move your weight forward on the machine and gently throttle back to reduce speed.

  Cornering weave occurs at lower speeds, which can surprise the unsuspecting rider. Again stability is restored by leaning forward to move your weight forward. Cornering weave is the more hazardous because it occurs when the machine is already destabilised by cornering forces.

Loading up the rear of the machine with luggage reduces the speed at which both types of weave occur. It is important to know the machines you ride so that you can anticipate the speeds, conditions and loadings which are likely to give rise to these types of instability.

Road, weather and traffic conditions

When you adapt your speed to the prevailing circumstances you must anticipate and plan for potential as well as actual dangers. This principle underlies all aspects of *Motorcycle Roadcraft* and is extensively covered in earlier chapters.

Speed limits

Statutory speed limits set the maximum permissible speed, but this is not the same thing as a safe speed. The safe speed for a particular stretch of road is determined by the conditions at the time. In winter, at night, in conditions of low visibility or high traffic volume the statutory speed limit may well be excessive. The onus is always on the rider to select a speed appropriate for the conditions.

Statutory maximum speed limits are not the same thing as the safe speed.

How speed affects the rider

Vision

As you ride faster, the nearest point at which you can accurately focus moves away from you. Foreground detail becomes blurred and observation becomes more difficult because you have to process more information in less time. The only way to cope with this is to scan further ahead, so that you gain more time to assess, plan and react. In complicated situations or where there is a lot of foreground information – in a busy shopping street, for example – you need to go more slowly to observe and process the information adequately.

See Chapter 3, ***Observation****, page 46,* ***How speed affects observation,*** *for more information.*

Underestimating speed

It is easy to underestimate the speed at which you are riding. Speed perception is complicated and depends on several factors such as:

- the difference in detail perceived by your forward and side vision
- the engine, road and wind noise
- the wind resistance on your chest and helmet
- the unevenness of the ride
- what you regard as a normal speed
- how wide the road is and whether it is enclosed or open
- your height off the ground.

Alterations to any of these factors can alter your perception of speed. The list that follows gives some common situations where speed perception can be distorted. The solution is simple – keep a check on your speedometer.

- When you have been travelling at high speed on a motorway or other fast road and then transfer to roads where speeds below 30 or 40 mph are appropriate, these lower speeds will seem much slower than they really are. Allow time for normal speed perception to return.

- When visibility is low – in fog, sleet, heavy rain and at night – speed perceptions become distorted and it is easy to ride faster than you realise.
- When riding a machine that is smoother, quieter or more powerful than your usual bike, it is easy to ride too fast. As well as sight and balance, you use other senses to assess speed: road noise, engine noise and vibration all play a part. When one or more of these is reduced, it can seem that you are going slower than you really are.
- On wide open roads, speeds will seem slower than on small confined roads.
- When you are fatigued.

See Chapter 1, *Becoming a better rider*, page 19, *Fatigue*.

Check your speedometer whenever you leave a motorway or high speed road.

Check your safety at speed

Over a journey of about one and a half hours, monitor whether you always ride so that you are able to stop on your own side of the road in the distance you can see to be clear.

Do you really know in practice what distance it will take you to stop at 20, 30, 40 and 50 mph? (See the *Highway Code*.)

Is there anywhere you can practise stopping from 70 mph in total safety?

If you do not keep to the safe stopping distance rule at higher speeds, why is this so?

Whatever the pressures to ride faster you must always ride within your own capabilities.

Using speed safely

The skill of riding safely at speed is not easily acquired. Every rider has their own speed limit: this is the highest speed at which they are safe and comfortable in any given situation. You should know what yours is and never go beyond it. At 30 mph a minor error may be corrected but at 70 mph the same error could be disastrous.

Speed must always be related to the extent of road you can see to be clear, and the ability to stop within this distance, by day or night. In this respect local knowledge, if wrongly used, can be hazardous because it can tempt you to ride faster than is safe along familiar roads.

You should know the braking characteristics of your bike and the table of stopping distances and be able to relate these to the road you are travelling on. Bear in mind that when speed is doubled braking distance quadruples, and that in wet and slippery conditions braking distances increase greatly.

See Chapter 4, ***Acceleration, using gears and braking****, page 80,* ***The safe stopping distance rule***

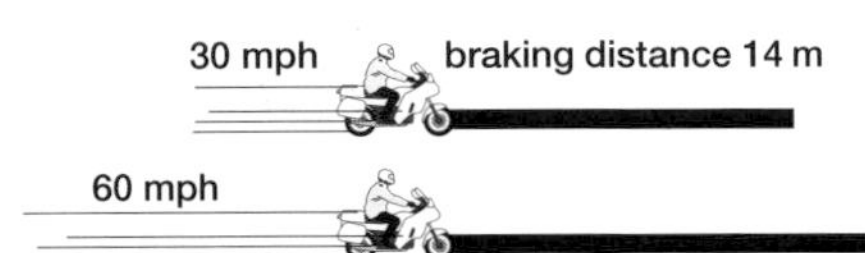

When speed is doubled, braking distance quadruples.

Overtaking

Riding at high speeds may entail frequent overtaking. Overtaking at speed demands careful preparation, positioning, observation and judgement of speed and distance. It is safest when carried out using the system of motorcycle control combined with a full awareness of possible hazards.

See Chapter 8, ***Overtaking****.*

Riding safely at speed depends above all else on adapting your speed to the circumstances. The faster you go the less time you have to react and the more disastrous the possible consequences.

Key safety points

These are the key points to remember:

- ride at a speed which is safe and at which you are confident and competent
- be familiar with the controls and the handling characteristics of your machine – use the controls smoothly
- high-speed riding requires maximum attentiveness – if you cannot achieve a high level of attentiveness because of fatigue or some other cause, do not ride
- always ride so that you can stop within the distance you can see to be clear, by day or by night
- if you double your speed you quadruple your braking distance
- put into practice the skills developed in *Motorcycle Roadcraft* which are designed to maximise safety
- be aware of the onset of fatigue, and take appropriate action
- no emergency is so great that it justifies an accident – it is far better to arrive late than not at all.

Review

In this chapter we have looked at:

- why speed affects safety
- how to assess a safe speed
- the factors which need to be considered when choosing the appropriate speed for the circumstances
- how speed affects the rider
- situations where it is difficult to assess speed correctly
- key points to help you ride safely at speed.

Check your understanding

Why do risks increase as you ride faster?

When is speed dangerous?

What is the safe stopping distance rule?

When does urgency justify taking risks?

Is it safe to ride at 30 mph in a built-up area?

Why do you need to ride more slowly in a busy shopping street?

Describe four situations where it can be difficult to assess speed accurately.

If you double your speed, by how much does your braking distance increase?

If you have difficulty in answering any of these questions, look back over the relevant part of this chapter to refresh your memory.

Appendices

Roadworthiness check

Before you start your journey you should ensure that your machine is roadworthy. Carry out the following checks:

- [ ] visual examination of the machine for damage, defects or leaks
- [ ] tools present and in good order
- [ ] wheels in good order and secure; spokes, if fitted, secure
- [ ] tyres – check both tyres for:
  - – damage
  - – tread depth and condition
  - – valve condition
  - – pressure (pressure settings are only accurate when tyres are cold; take into account whether you will be riding solo or not)
  - – compatibility of type
- [ ] adequate fuel, oil, water and other fluids
- [ ] luggage and panniers secure and well balanced
- [ ] lights – including high intensity foglight, day running lights, indicators and brakelight – in working order
- [ ] steering head moves freely from lock to lock
- [ ] horn working correctly
- [ ] foot rests in good order
- [ ] all glass clean – lenses, mirrors and windshield
- [ ] visor clean and scratch free, treated with anti-mist spray if appropriate
- [ ] helmet undamaged and well-fitting
- [ ] drive chain in good condition and properly adjusted
- [ ] suspension settings suitably adjusted.

A useful aid to remember the key points to check is:

P	**O**	**W**	**E**	**R**
petrol	oil	water	electrics	rubber (tyres)

Pre-riding check

Carry out this check every time you ride a motorcycle. Make sure you are familiar with the position and operation of the controls and instruments before setting off:

- [ ] remove machine from stand and ensure that stand is fully retracted
- [ ] check that the gear is in neutral
- [ ] identify additional riding aids (ABS, traction control, linked brakes)
- [ ] check and adjust position of controls where possible
- [ ] check brakes for operation
- [ ] number and position of gears.

Turn on the fuel if necessary
Set the manual choke if necessary
Switch on the ignition
Note the warning lights
Start the engine.

Continue with these checks:

- [ ] after engine starts recheck the instruments
- [ ] adjust mirrors to give best view
- [ ] make sure all the auxiliaries are working
- [ ] check gauges and warning lights
- [ ] check in mirror, select gear, check all round and move off when safe.

As soon as possible after moving off carry out a moving brake test (see page 80). Check the gauges and warning lights at intervals during the journey; take action if necessary.

Glossary

Acceleration sense
The ability to vary vehicle speed in response to changing road and traffic conditions by accurate use of the throttle. *See page 68*

Antilock braking system (ABS)
A braking system which prevents the wheels locking during harsh or emergency braking. Also known as ABS. *See page 99*

Aquaplaning
A serious loss of steering and braking control caused by a wedge of water building up between the front tyre and the road surface. *See page 105*

Auxiliaries
The auxiliary controls on a vehicle as distinct from the major controls. Examples of the auxiliaries are: horn, indicators and lights. *See Controls, Instruments*

Blind spots
Areas around a machine which the rider cannot see because the mirrors do not cover them. *See page 45,49*

Camber
The convex slope across a road surface designed to assist drainage. Camber falls from the crown of the road to the edges. It has an effect on cornering which differs according to whether the bend is to the right or the left. *See page 89*

Controls
The major controls of a motorcycle are the throttle, brakes, clutch, gear lever and handlebars. *See Auxiliaries, Instruments*

Cornering
Cornering is used to mean riding a machine round a corner, curve or bend. Its meaning is not restricted to corners. *See Chapter 5*

Cylinder compression
See Engine compression

Engine compression
The compression of gases in the cylinders of an internal combustion engine. Compression uses energy so, when deceleration reduces the fuel supply to the engine, energy for compression is taken from the rear wheel, thereby slowing it down.

Engine torque
The turning power developed by an engine.

Following position
The distance at which it is safe to follow a vehicle in front. This distance varies according to the circumstances. *See pages 82, 120, 129*

Gears
The mechanism which converts the engine output into different speed and power combinations at the rear wheel. A high gear is a gear which drives the rear wheel faster; a low gear is a gear which drives the rear wheel more slowly. Top gear is the highest gear; bottom gear is the lowest gear.

Hazard/hazardous
Any thing or situation that has the potential for danger. *See page 28*

Information phase
First phase of the system of motorcycle control which underlies the other phases. *See page 30*

Instruments
The gauges, dials, warning lights, etc of a machine that give information about how it is functioning: for example, the speedometer, oil warning light and main beam indicator. *See Auxiliaries, Controls*

Lifesaver
A final glance backwards into a blind area before committing yourself to a manoeuvre. As the name suggests it could save your life. *See page 31.*

Limit point
The limit point is the furthest point along a road to which you have an uninterrupted view of the road surface. On a level stretch of road this will be where the right-hand side of the road appears to intersect with the left-hand side of the road. The limit point is used in a system of cornering called limit point analysis. *See page 91*

Nearside
The left side of a machine, vehicle or animal looking forward from the rider's position.

Offside
The right side of a machine, vehicle or animal looking forward from the rider's position.

Overtaking position
The position adopted behind another vehicle in readiness to overtake when a safe opportunity arises. It is usually closer than the following position and reduces the time you have to react to actions of the vehicle in front. *See page 131*

POWER check
An aid for remembering the key items to check before starting a journey:
Petrol Oil Water Electrics Rubber (tyres). *See page 147*

Red mist
A mental and physiological state which riders experience when they are so determined to achieve some non-riding objective, such as pursuing a vehicle in front, that they are no longer capable of assessing riding risks realistically. It is associated with a greatly increased accident risk. *See page 8*

Revs
The number of engine revolutions per minute.

Rev limiter
A mechanism fitted to some machines which restricts over-revving of the engine.

Road users
Any user of the highway: riders, drivers, cyclists, pedestrians, animals.

Roadside marker posts
Posts marking the edge of the road, displaying red reflective studs on the nearside of the road and white reflective studs on the offside of the road.

Safe stopping distance rule
This rule is one of the basic safety considerations when riding. It controls your speed by relating speed to the ability to stop. Always ride so that you are able to stop on your own side of the road in the distance you can see to be clear. *See page 80*

Scanning
Method of observation. The use of regular visual sweeps of the whole of the riding environment – the distance, the mid-ground, the foreground, sides and rear, including mirrors – to ensure that the rider is aware of everything that is happening. *See pages 17,44* Ed note: correction to Pilot edition page numbers

Superelevation
The banking up of a section of road towards the outside edge of the curve. This makes the slope favourable for cornering in both directions. *See page 89*

The system – the system of motorcycle control
A systematic way of approaching and negotiating hazards that emphasises safety and is central to *Motorcycle Roadcraft*.
See Chapter 2

Traction
The grip of a tyre on the road surface.

Traction control systems
Traction control improves vehicle stability by controlling excess wheel slip on the rear wheel during acceleration. *See page 99*

Tyre grip trade-off
The tyre grip available in any given situation is limited, and is shared between accelerating, braking and cornering forces. If more of the tyre grip is used for braking or accelerating, less will be available for cornering. *See pages 65, 86*

Wheel slip
The difference between the velocity of the vehicle and the velocity of the outer circumference of the tyre, usually expressed as a percentage.

Index